ALLERTON PARK INSTITUTE
Number 33

Papers Presented at the Allerton Park Institute

Sponsored by

University of Illinois
Graduate School of Library and Information Science

held

October 27-29, 1991
Allerton Conference Center
Robert Allerton Park
Monticello, Illinois

Applying Research to Practice
How to Use Data Collection and Research to Improve Library Management Decision Making

LEIGH STEWART ESTABROOK

Editor

University of Illinois
Graduate School of Library and Information Science
Urbana-Champaign, Illinois

Printed in the United States of America on Acid-Free Paper

CONTENTS

Introduction

The Allerton Park Conference on "Applying Research to Practice" marked the anniversary of the founding of the Library Research Center 30 years earlier. The Library Research Center (LRC) was established in 1961 by Robert Downs with an LSCA grant from the Illinois State Library for the purpose of establishing an experimental center for research related to public library development. That early grant helped shape the LRC's ongoing concern for conducting research that can be applied directly to solving problems of practice.

In this age of declining resources with constant demands for accountability and productivity, an increasing number of librarians have become researchers and use research in their work. As a result, the LRC has assumed a larger teaching role. On behalf of the Illinois State Library and other professional associations, its staff have led workshops for practicing librarians on such topics as data collection, community analysis, and statistical methods. This Allerton Conference was developed as part of that teaching mission. Papers were focused on topics that could help participants become better consumers of research, understand new ways in which research can help their libraries, and be more informed collaborators in the research process. Participants in the conference also had the opportunity to meet informally to discuss research problems in their individual libraries. Unfortunately, we have no way to represent the important content of these discussions in this printed volume.

Glenn Holt, Director of the St. Louis Public Library, offered an impassioned keynote presentation in which he argued that research is a policy-making imperative for public library practitioners. Too often, he states, staff make assumptions about their public that are not true. For example, contrary to staff assumptions, there was a broad base of support for a library tax increase among St. Louis residents who then voted for a significant increase in the Library's tax base.

Holt notes the relatively small number of researchers within schools of library and information science at the same time the need for such research is increasing. Research has become an important part of the operations of St. Louis Public Library, and the paper summarizes some of its recent projects. Holt concludes his paper with a call for greater collaboration among public library researchers and for a second Public Library Inquiry as a way of inspiring new commitment to research within the practitioner community.

The paper by Keith Lance and Katy Sherlock provides an example of one area in which librarians have collaborated for many years— collection and distribution of library statistics. The National Center for Educational Statistics, state libraries, and others are a rich source of data about communities, collection, services, and other factual information. Lance and Sherlock summarize the basic types of information available and then address the types of issues that might be addressed by different types of data and the important question of how these data can be used by managers.

Nancy Van House addresses one of the key areas for which data are collected and for which librarians are held accountable: evaluation. She suggests that libraries use evaluation for internal decision making and communication with the external environment. Among the important issues she raises is the way in which library values come into play in evaluation, either explicitly or implicitly. What is valued by a library may differ from what is valued by any one of its constituent groups. What a library chooses to evaluate (types of users, fill rate, response time) indicates what it deems important. Van House outlines the data or objective evidence on which libraries can evaluate themselves. She concludes with a brief discussion of the use of evaluation.

Joe Spaeth, a sociologist affiliated with the University of Illinois' Survey Research Laboratory, presents a practical and detailed discussion of perils and pitfalls of survey research. Community and user surveys are the most common forms of original research employed in libraries. Spaeth covers the stages involved in surveys from research designs through sampling, questionnaire construction, data collection, processing, analysis, and reporting. He also examines advantages and disadvantages of mail, face-to-face, and telephone surveys.

An important theme of Jane B. Robbins' paper is the value of communication between researchers and practitioners. Noting the bifurcation of the research and practitioner communities in many fields, Robbins addresses ways in which they may be brought together within librarianship. Among her recommendations are (a) educating practitioners to become knowledgeable consumers of research/knowledge production and (b) encouraging researchers to make their findings more accessible by publishing in journals read by practitioners and writing in clear, direct language.

Robbins is concerned also with research carried out by practitioners, much of which is never published. Noting the importance of making research findings available to a larger audience, she provides suggestions that help practitioners communicate their findings more effectively.

Drawing on her own research focus, Margaret Kimmel directs her comments to issues in research on youth services in libraries. She cites encouraging new efforts to collect data about young library users, but notes the lack of a theoretical framework for analysis or critical mass of researchers concerned with this area. Kimmel points to important research by Schorr and Heath—both from other disciplines—which can provide important insights to librarians. At the same time, Kimmel provides discouraging examples of ways in which libraries have not used the findings of research or been willing to conduct further research to improve their quality of service.

Beginning with a question about the difference between "ordinary knowledge" and research, J. R. Bradley asks her audience to consider how members can translate their observations of and questions about the physical world into a focus for research. Bradley is concerned with the complexity of the issues librarians wish to understand and the difficulties in collecting and analyzing data in ways that do not bias or oversimplify our understanding of those issues. The questions she raises are indeed complicated but nonetheless important; and they underlie many of the points raised in other papers, particularly those by Van House, Spaeth, and Cronin.

A complement to Bradley's, Blaise Cronin's paper suggests that problems become research problems when individuals become curious about unanswered questions that can be subjected to systematic investigation and verification by reputable and credible individuals. Cronin presents a brief summary of research in a Fortune 500 company and suggests how individuals might structure their research. He then summarizes common pitfalls of researchers. Cronin concludes with personal reflection that good researchers will have curiosity, passion, and a deep knowledge of their field.

Debra Johnson, who worked for several years with the Library Research Center, presented the final paper of the conference: an exploration of the various roles in the research process. Actors in the research process include not only individual practitioners and researchers, but also state library agencies, consultants, professional associations, research firms, and users. Johnson provides examples of ways in which members of each of these groups can be important in idea generating, data collecting, and producing and consuming research.

The conference concluded with a panel discussion by three individuals knowledgeable about funding for research. A summary of the comments by Dwight Burlingame, W. David Penniman, and Gail McClure conclude this volume.

LEIGH STEWART ESTABROOK
Editor

GLEN E. HOLT

Executive Director
St. Louis Public Library
St. Louis, Missouri

Research for Change: Creating Strategic Futures for Public Libraries

ABSTRACT

Research is a policy-making imperative for public library practitioners. It helps them understand the cognitive errors that limit their operation, establish a policy framework for their operations, and assess operational efficiency and effectiveness. A growing insufficiency of applied or action research on public libraries creates the need for practitioners to undertake studies themselves. This need is greater because of rapid demographic, economic, and cultural changes associated with the information age. These changes—and public library responses to them—are explored in some detail. The research projects of the St. Louis Public Library are summarized. The article ends with an invitation for cooperation to obtain more research on public libraries and a call for a second Public Library Inquiry as an appropriate mechanism to inspire new commitment to such research.

INTRODUCTION

"How we know what isn't so." That's the title of a recent book by psychologist Thomas Gilovich (1991). Gilovich's specialty is human cognitive error. In other words, he studies how and why people make mistakes when they think about their world.

Gilovich shows that all of us make errors. Sometimes these errors are nothing short of monumental. Francis Bacon thought that warts

5

could be cured by rubbing them with pork. And Aristotle thought that male babies were conceived in a strong north wind. Gilovich's book contains many more examples.

Sometimes we make cognitive errors on the job. If these misperceptions dominate the institutional culture, organizations work poorly (Bolman & Deal, 1991, pts. 5 and 6). If the errors are of sufficient magnitude, they can imperil an institution's future.

When I came to direct the St. Louis Public Library (SLPL) in April 1987, management staff portrayed institutional culture almost entirely in negative terms. For them, the future appeared grim. Here are four of the claims they made:

1. Library customers used only one branch, the one closest to their home, almost always walking there. If the library closed any branch, that circulation was lost forever.
2. Over 40 percent of Central Library visitors were noncity residents who provided no financial support to the institution.
3. Not many business persons used the library because they had their own sources of information.
4. Conservative St. Louisans, who had voted down most citywide tax increases since 1971, the year of the library's last successful levy election, would never increase tax support for the library.

Between 1987 and 1991, various SLPL research projects (all of which are listed in the Appendix) demonstrated that each of these assertions involved human cognitive error:

1. A branch services study (1990) demonstrated that most library customers shopped at two or three branches and that circulation could be transferred.
2. Regular surveys of walk-in and telephone users (1990-1991) demonstrated that less than 20 percent of all Central Library visitors were nonresidents.
3. A business users survey (1990) demonstrated that the principal reason that business researchers did not use SLPL was because they did not know about its information services. The study showed that a latent market existed for the library's information services to business.
4. A series of constituency analyses (October 1987, January-March 1987, October 1990) revealed a broad base of support for a library tax increase. These surveys translated into a 61 percent vote for a March 1988 tax referendum, which nearly doubled the library's tax base.

If public library leaders want to chart a strategic future for their institutions, they must begin by creating a climate in which that change can take place (Waterman, 1987). Research is a tool to help define the human cognitive errors that keep an institution from developing its strategic future.

RESEARCH TO DEFINE INSTITUTIONAL PLACE

Research to sort out cognitive errors involves analysis of institutional culture. Formulation of an institutional rationale entails asking a different set of questions, those that relate to its environment (context), the character of its operations, and its roles.

Here are four questions worth asking while attempting to develop a strategic rationale:

1. What expectations are realistic given budget and staff size? In fiscal year 1990, the seven largest public libraries in the United States each spent over $40 million, but only 8 percent managed a budget of more than $1 million. Seventeen percent had a budget less than $10,000. Ten percent (910) of all public library districts served 72 percent of the population. Ninety percent (8,058 systems) attended the remaining 28 percent. Only 10 percent of all public libraries had over 25 staff members. Twenty-five percent had less than one paid full-time staff member (Public Library Association, 1991, pp. 17-28; Podolsky, 1991, p. iii).
2. What is the socioeconomic character of the community served? At a recent PLA workshop, Michael J. Weiss (1988, 1989) suggested that American communities can be sorted into forty "neighborhood types." Applications of techniques like those utilized by Weiss may help a public library comprehend the community to be served.
3. What is the financial setting in which the library functions? Most public libraries remain 85 percent to 95 percent locally funded and compete for support with other public services like schools, police, and sewers (Prottas, 1981; Trezza, 1989). Affecting the ability to deal with this competition is the particular ideology of public finance that dominates the thinking of a library's administration or its board (Robinson, 1989).
4. Of what significance is an institution's role as a legatee institution? Like public schools, public libraries are legatee (inheritor) institutions. As knowledge has broadened and as society's needs have changed, public libraries have taken on new jobs.

The public library is, first, the legatee of subject types. Public libraries began as repositories of useful knowledge. As the world grew more specialized, so too did their collections.

The public library, second, is the legatee of changing formats. After books came microforms, 16-millimeter film, videotapes, CDs, and other electronic formats. If a format exists, public libraries usually try to collect it.

Third, the public library serves as a legatee of functions. Because public libraries engage in community library service, local governments ask them to register voters. Because they circulate children's books, some parents expect them to baby-sit and to offer specialized day care for latchkey children. Because they offer books and information on learning to read, corporate America expects them to help illiterates learn to read.

To sum up, whether the public library legacy has involved subject matter, formats, or functions, the result has been additive. This additive, legatee character may not serve public libraries well in the current "age of convergence" (Wedgeworth, 1991). This age, according to Robert Wedgeworth, is one where firms from one information technology sector broaden their business to compete with those in other sectors. In the process, private companies probably will begin to compete with some services offered by public libraries.

How should legatee public libraries act in an age of convergence? Some already are repositioning themselves for new kinds of competition. Others appear oblivious of the convergence trend.

Research to create an institutional rationale creates a sense of how one public library fits among the many and locates the institution within the community context. Asking the kinds of questions posed in this section usually is part of that research.

A SEARCH FOR SUFFICIENCY

It is hard to read very much library science research literature without encountering a variety of articles discussing its demerits. Among those authors criticizing library research and researchers are Freeman (1985), Childers (1984), Converse (1984), Schlachter (1989), and Van House (1991). Public library practitioners must not become obsessive in their attention to this criticism.

When practitioners search for research literature that addresses operational and policy concerns, their principal criticism usually is that an appropriate article does not exist. The research article they would most like to have is the one that has not yet been written.

This fact should not be surprising. The practice of librarianship generates a huge research need, yet the number who write to meet that need is very small. Charles McClure and Ann Bishop (1989) suggest that no more than 300 "active researchers" furnish the critical research foundation for the work of a labor force of 153,000 in a business dominated by books, journals, and electronic information.

Public library practitioners do little formal publishing to meet their own research needs. Keith Swigger (1985) found that library school faculty, comprising slightly "less than one percent of the professional community—authored over 23 percent of the articles" (p. 105). Academic librarians authored 30 percent of the articles. Public librarians contributed less than 9 percent of the total research. Swigger's findings are substantiated by Watson (1985). Current trends make it improbable that public librarians can rely on library school faculty to increase public library research because the number of such scholars is shrinking.

Fourteen library schools have closed since 1978, reducing library science faculty opportunities. In 1975-1976, 67 library schools had 648 full-time faculty. In 1985-1986, 64 schools had 562 faculty (Biggs, 1991, esp. p. 37, n. 7). The loss of schools in this comparison amounted to 4.5 percent. The loss of faculty was 13.3 percent, indicating that some relatively large library schools had been shut down.

Even at schools still open, replacement faculty, especially those in growth fields, are in short supply. Doctoral output is dropping, with the ability to replace aging faculty becoming problematical (Futas & Zipkowitz, 1991). The continuing "Darwinism at the University," which has forced library school closings, seems likely to continue (Stieg, 1991). Because of these trends, public library practitioners face the prospect that they increasingly will have to undertake the research that needs to be done.

ACTION RESEARCH

Practitioner research, in reality, already is a significant fact in the United States and Great Britain. Recent examples include D'Elia (1991); Smulyan (1989); Sunnydale, CA (1990); Milwaukee Public Library (1987); Enoch Pratt Free Library (1989); Franks (1991); Lyman, Slater, and Walker (1982, p. 40 & passim).

Practitioners undertake research for different reasons than library school faculty. Reflecting this difference, practitioner research is usually labeled "applied research." Robert Swisher and Charles McClure, reflecting the typical policy orientation of practitioner research, call it "action research" (Swisher & McClure, 1984).

Swisher and McClure (1984, p. 14) articulate four rationales for action research. Following each item is my listing of institutional research activities which that particular rationale statement seems to justify.

1. Test "traditional assumptions of library services and activities." This rationale covers tests for service quality, user surveys, staffing assessments, training surveys, and operations measurements.
2. Establish and measure "goals and objectives, accountability, and justify library activities." This rationale covers the development of mission statements, plans, and accountability studies.
3. Measure "effectiveness and efficiency, and select which of the two is to be maximized for individual library programs." This rationale allows service-level assessments, input-output analysis, cost accounting, and cost-benefit analysis.
4. Measure "environmental change . . . [a]s a natural, ongoing occurrence." This rationale encompasses environmental scanning as part of strategic planning, demographic assessments, user assessments, support assessments, and marketing studies.

To the Swisher and McClure list, I add one other rationale that is of growing importance in public library management:

5. Research to add value. This rationale allows creating new access points to the collection, product development, donor research, and development of funding proposals. Special libraries already have begun to add value as an explicit part of their professional purpose (Bender, 1991). Public (and academic) libraries will follow.

These five rationales justify a variety of practitioner studies. The need for such studies exists even without rapid change. With change running at seatide, an even greater need exists to undertake institutional research to help create strategic futures for modern public libraries.

A SEATIDE OF CHANGE—FUTURE TRENDS

Six major trends add to the imperative for action research. Futurist Joel Barker (1991) speaks of these momentous changes as paradigm shifts. Definitionally expanded and popularized by Thomas Kuhn (1962), a paradigm is a fixed form or set of forms. In culture, whether for a whole society, one of its institutional sectors, or for a single organization, a paradigm shift occurs when old forms break down and thereby change the rules for doing business.

Here are six major trends that are breaking down the old rules for conducting the business of public libraries. Along with the specific references cited, this section draws from Snyder and Edwards (1991), Research Alert (1991), Cetron and Davies (1990), Toffler (1990), Naisbitt and Aburdene (1990), United Way (1988, 1990), and Kidder (1987). It also draws on the literature on library futures, including Mason (1985),

Blodgett (1986), U.S. Department of Education (1987), OCLC (1988), Epstein (1989), Garfield (1988), Summers (1989), Furthering the Vision (1989), and Croneberger (1989).

1. *Globalization of Information Culture.* Instant electronic communication has created "the global village." The shift is exemplified by wars fought on CNN and a battered American economy that reacts to news from Moscow, Berlin, and Tokyo. "Currency" (instant access) of information is the hallmark of global-village culture. Those without such access become information have-nots who are unable to compete or even to react because they do not know that anything is happening.

2. *Innovations in Information Technology Will Remain the Driving Force (the Independent Variable) in Exponential Change.* Television, personal computers, CD-ROMs, and faxes all created turmoil in old markets and brought rapid development of new businesses. A massive latent market for current information still remains untapped, and markets already served by one information form will be served by newer, more convenient forms.

3. *Increased Competition for Public Funding.* In recent decades, the public economy has become more competitive at all governmental levels. All agencies, including public libraries, will have to compete for resources at every level. When competition for funding is severe, demands for accountability and increased productivity increase. Calls will increase for public libraries to add value and to share resources.

4a. *The American Population is Changing through Demographic Shifts.* By the year 2000, "80% of all mothers will have a career during some portion of their child-rearing years," and "85% of work force entrants will be minorities, women, and new immigrants" (Vanderkolk & Young, 1991, pp. 11, 20). People live farther from work, with average commuting time expected to double through the 1990s. More families have made it into the "upper one-fifth" income category, but the middle class is shrinking: About one-fifth of all families (and one-fourth of all children) live below the poverty line (Gallagher, 1991). Fewer persons reside in traditional families, and more persons, including increasing numbers of the elderly, live alone. Varied birthrates (and migration) will make Hispanic Americans the largest U.S. ethnic and racial minority by 2000. Other nonwhite groups, including African-Americans, are increasing as well.

4b. *The American Population is Changing through Migration.* America's population is rearranging itself. Employment is becoming more footloose, creating significant inter-regional shifts in the location of jobs. Regions (and areas within regions) with high amenity levels (including physical newness) are attracting inhabitants. The populations of inner cities are becoming both older and younger, with higher percentages of minorities and those with literacy problems. Edge cities are growing on the rims of old metropolitan areas. Exurban (on the periphery of metropolitan areas) population is increasing. Large sections of American urban areas are coming to be dominated by multicultural groups different from prevailing white culture.

5. *Increasing Alternatives to the Public Library.* New information technology access combinations—the growth of CompuServe and Prodigy, Sony electronic books, and CD-ROM libraries on disk— have appeared in the last half decade. These new "library" or information-source alternatives represent the edge of new kinds of competition for the public library's information and reading customers. That is especially true for upper- and middle-income users who will be presented with information and book-acquiring options that do not involve going to the public library.

6. *Library School Teaching and Research Positions Will Continue to be Affected Negatively by Changes in the Academy.* American universities have become less regional and more national, less oriented to the service professions and more centered on "pure research," and more conscious of needing "bottom-line" departments that generate high national visibility, significant research income, and high levels of donor support. Library schools historically fit on the regional- and local-service side of the new academic equation, and many have closed. As this trend continues, public library practitioners will have to deal with the implications of fewer library science researchers and fewer schools where librarians can receive their MLS training.

PREDICTED PUBLIC LIBRARY RESPONSES TO FUTURE TRENDS

For public libraries, paradigm shifts in the critical environment signal a need for an institution to shift its goals, constituencies, or ways of doing business. Barker (1991) suggests that unless an institution makes such shifts, it faces the prospect of becoming absolutely or relatively less useful. If it does not adjust, it eventually will lose its claim to resources. Paradigm shifts also flag a management challenge: to adapt in an appropriate way and at just the right time so that resource use can be optimized.

Institutional change in libraries is a continuous process. Many authors have written about changes currently taking place in public libraries and about those expected to take place. In the paragraphs that follow, I have attempted to summarize a large amount of literature dealing with current and seemingly imminent shifts in public libraries associated with the momentous and rapid changes—the paradigm shifts—already occurring in the world and in the United States.

Responses to Economic Pressures

Consolidation

Consolidation to obtain service efficiencies and to cut costs already has occurred in financial institutions (Dealers Return, 1991) and information companies (Goldstein, 1990, p. 330). The public library field contains a large group of chronically underfunded institutions with low levels of capitalization and no case reserve. To remain independent and still serve their users well, such institutions must find income to pay for electronic access. Meanwhile, information technology makes cooperative arrangements easier. A shrinking of branch-outlet numbers and the joining of underfunded library districts seems a likely scenario through the 1990s.

Resource Sharing

Along with the possibility of consolidation, many public libraries will face pressure to share resources (Sherman & Sanders, 1989, pp. 143-144). At the national level, NREN (National Research and Education Network) legislation will impact public libraries, even though profound funding and operating issues remain unresolved (Corbin, 1991; McClure, Bishop, Doty, & Rosenbaum, 1990). Poorer district, interlibrary loan (ILL) demand will escalate exponentially, with net-lenders initiating policies to deal with inequities in borrowing versus ability to pay (Sager, 1991; OCLC, 1990; Ballard, 1990). Questions about the appropriateness of ILL requests will become sharper and louder. An important new resource-sharing issue is the organization of "just-in-time delivery" as the need for materials currency increases and as libraries cut back on their purchases in anticipation of sharing resources. Reciprocal borrowing agreements also can be expected to proliferate, probably to the detriment of library districts that are unable to enter such agreements (Sherman & Sanders, 1989, pp. 140-143).

Cross-type Library Cooperation

The "official" barriers retarding and even prohibiting cooperation between "types" of libraries, including those involving no governmental funding, will break down through the 1990s (Townley, 1989). Public library cooperation with schools and colleges will grow in significance (Beach, 1989).

Partnerships

Public libraries will form extensive partnerships with nonlibrary institutions and private corporations. "Teletext, videotext, and videodisk technologies hold great promise for cooperation between the public and private sector" (Sager, 1981, p. 309). Single-function partnering also has appeared among libraries. One example is the Philadelphia Area Consortium of Special Collections Libraries cataloging project involving sixteen Philadelphia institutions (Holdings, 1991).

New kinds of public-private partnerships will appear through the 1990s. IBM and the "Baby-Bells" are the biggest and best-known among current public library partners, co-developing products and protocols that offer greater access or add to service levels in libraries throughout the United States.

Flattening of Library Hierarchy

Well-funded suburban and small-town community libraries will purchase access to sophisticated electronic information networks, reducing their customers' need to travel to large city or university libraries to gain access to certain research collections (Blegan, 1990). Unless federal and state governments, historically those most concerned with equity issues in resources, furnish support, those people who reside in public library districts without resources will be disadvantaged even more because they will not have access to information sources.

Collections and Programmatic Responses

Some of these traditions are old, but these areas often gain nuances in response to the forces of change.

Books

"The book will remain a key instrument for the preservation of historical, cultural, and social knowledge," Ken Dowlin (1986) writes. "Yet, we will need to enhance its viability by expanding the retrievability of the knowledge contained within" (p. 5). "Books will still be the predominant medium in most libraries," and, combined with computers, they will be used to create what Dowlin (1991) calls the ideal library, "a library with the ambiance and sense of community of a small town with instantaneous global communications" (p. 5). Computers will be used to print books on demand (O'Brien, 1989, p. 29). The cost of books remains an important factor in any future equation (Mason, 1991, pp. 2-3, 7-10).

Business Users

Public libraries will expand their efforts to help business constituents, especially those in small businesses, to compete in a world market. Some already have begun to enhance services to businesses. Home office workers, "America's fastest growing work force," present a special opportunity (Working from Home, 1991).

Special Constituencies

Demands for library services for special populations are bound to increase. The recently passed Americans with Disabilities Act (PL 101-336) is not a suggestion but a demand for services that public libraries will have to meet (Gunde, 1991). Foreign-language speakers, most especially Hispanics, will have new and heavier reading needs. The elderly require special services. Those involved in distance education and in-home schooling will make greater demands (LaRue & LaRue, 1991). Poorer Americans, especially nonwhites, have special library and information needs, including the need for access to government information (Berman, 1990). Responding to special populations requires the public library to be more proactive in serving those populations (Panz, 1989, pp. 151-171; Sherrill, 1970, p. 34). That means operating in nontraditional ways, often away from library buildings.

Consumer, Environmental, and Volunteer Association Information

As deregulation of business has freed up competition in many market sectors, consumers want more information on companies and products in order to protect themselves. As volunteerism has received renewed emphasis, associations and organizations of volunteers, without large capital resources, turn to the public library for information of all types (Westin & Finger, 1991, pp. 4-5, 40-42).

Literacy Collections and Programs

New Orleans Public has literacy instructors on staff, and several systems support PALS (Project for Automated Library System) computer-assisted, literacy-tutoring learning stations as part of their regular library operations. Others have begun or are beginning family literacy programs.

Training in Information Handling and Searching

Some public libraries can respond to a significant latent market for training in information handling and searching by contracting to train private sector company employees in database management. A University of Missouri School of Library and Information Science course in reference methods taught in St. Louis this fall attracted nearly 50 percent of its enrollees from persons looking for help with their jobs. This demand constitutes a new (or at least an increased) adult education need with which at least some public libraries will be asked to deal.

More Service and Less Place Oriented

"In the evolving electronic era, the public library is becoming less a place than a service" (Westin & Finger, 1991, p. 55). Easy access to information through technology has brought library output to "a greater emphasis on the provision of information rather than provision of the material" (Perry, 1986, p. 7). At the same time, public librarians will follow their museum colleagues in paying more attention to service quality (Sorensen, 1989; Wright, 1989).

Children's Services

Children's services will receive greater emphasis because public libraries will react to the reality that childhood has changed. Richard Louv (1990) writes that childhood has been redefined by a broad "expansion of experience and the contraction of positive adult contact . . . . Children and adults pass each other in the night at ever-accelerating speeds, and the American social environment becomes increasingly lonely for both" (p. 5). Public libraries will be looked to as "the last safe place" and as volunteer "family hubs" that will take on surrogate school and parent roles (pp. 325-329). This shift will make children and students—along with researchers and pleasure readers—the primary in-building users of libraries (O'Brien, 1989, p. 29).

Responsive Use of Resources within Libraries

Information Technology Changes Library Work

Technology historian Derek de Solla Price (1980), commenting on the arrival of computers in libraries, notes, "A new technology never just replaces the old method—it enables quite different styles of life to come into being" (p. 14).

The computer already has changed information agency work-styles (Information Technology, 1991; Zuboff, 1988; Siegel, 1991). It has enhanced frequent-user expectations about what they can find and reference librarians' anticipations of the help they will be able to provide. Librarians also will assume new evaluative and directive information roles (Nitecki, 1983; Smith, 1991; Young, 1989, pp. 7-10; Whitlatch, 1991).

"Information is data endowed with relevance and purpose. Converting data into information thus requires knowledge. And knowledge, by definition, is specialized" (Drucker, 1988, p. 46). To deal with this reality, public library professional staff will assume new evaluative and directive roles and practice "critical librarianship," becoming "mediators" (or "navigators") who develop "cognitive maps" to improve individual access in anticipation of customer need (Blegan, 1990, pp. 464-465; Wurman, 1989, pp. 45-50; Webster, 1987, pp. 173-189; Malinconico, 1989, pp. 142-144; Summers, 1989, pp. 25-30).

Measuring Productivity and Defining Output

The composition of library staff is changing, with increasing numbers of nonlibrarian computer programmers, information professionals, service para-professionals, and clerks involved in shaping public access to library materials and information databases (Penniman, 1991a, 1991b; Young, 1989). These shifts suggest the need to redefine professional library work. They also suggest a need to develop more comprehensive statistical methods than those suggested in Van House, Lynch, McClure, Zweizig, & Rodger (1987) to measure public library productivity. The shifts also suggest a need for new attention to the ethics of librarianship.

Productivity—Staff Education

To meet the pressure for improved productivity, public libraries are following private sector corporations and spending more money to improve the quality of their work forces through education (Patterson, 1991; Altman & Brown, 1991; Marchant & England, 1989; Zuboff, 1985). Large public libraries can be expected to start or enlarge their in-service education function dramatically over the next decade (Cargill & Webb, 1988, pp. 113-141).

Productivity—Exported and Shared Jobs

Larger public libraries are likely to follow the lead of the National Library of Medicine, which contracts with abstractors, and McGraw-Hill, which employs clerical help working in Ireland (Wysocki, 1991). Public library cataloging probably will be the first library function to move not only off-site but in many cases out of system.

Competition for Top-Notch Professional Staff

Quality information professionals, especially women who make up a majority of most public library professional staff, will be in high demand through the next decade. Public library management will have to respond to the needs of this work group, who want higher salaries, pay equity, child care, and flexible hours, along with self-actualization on the job (Yankelovich, 1981). More generally, one futurist writes, "This means that people don't have to put up with management stupidity. Their attitude now can be 'Shape up or I ship out'" (Thornburg, 1991, p. 41).

Although library managers "will become more conciliatory, collaborative, and team oriented" (Thornburg, 1991, p. 41), they also will become increasingly self-conscious about the productivity of staff. That means not paying high professional salaries to just anybody. "The ratio of support staff to professional staff should continue to increase from 2 to 1 to 4 or 5 to 1, minimizing an organization's need to replace each professional with another professional" (Cargill & Webb, 1988, p. 162). Pay-for-performance programs also can be expected to increase in public libraries (St. Louis Public Library, 1990).

Minority Employment

The overall public library record on the recruitment and retention of minority employees is less than cause for a celebration. Given the current and probable national legislative and court situation, the main effort to recruit, train, and promote minorities will occur in a few states and some local systems. The arrival of well-educated, foreign-born professionals will affect libraries' minority-recruitment pattern.

Technology Investment

In the past twenty years, this nation has invested a trillion dollars in computers and communications technology, with only small increases in productivity (Snyder & Edwards, 1991, pp. 10-11). We should see a productivity payoff beginning in this decade, but most public libraries will continue to invest in new technology so staff and customers can have access to numerous current databases that are relatively easy to search. In the words of futurist Joseph F. Coates, "Smart companies will pour capital into their businesses; dumb companies will tighten their belts" (Thornburg, 1991, p. 39). Public libraries that do not invest in technology risk limiting future options.

Measurements of Accountability and Institutional Development

Cost Accounting

The old adage, "What you don't know can't hurt you" is no longer true. To present viable policy alternatives to boards of directors, library policy makers need to know the costs of new programs and those to be supplemented or replaced. More effective management will require effective accounting systems that can track work functions. During the 1990s, many public libraries will see the introduction of true cost accounting in order to place dollar value on the delivery of particular services.

Ascertaining Value Added and Planning Resource Use

One specialized aspect of cost accounting is ascertaining value produced by public investment (Snyder & Edwards, 1991, p. 10). During the 1990s, to keep up with other information agencies, many public libraries will devise mechanisms to measure effectively the value they add to area economies. Before the end of the decade, most larger public libraries will join other public services and cultural institutions in offering their financial supporters an analysis of their costs and benefits. Snyder makes the point for information firms generally. It seems obviously relevant. We also will develop measurements by which we can talk about benefits-to-cost ratios of our library expenditures.

Measuring Services and Users

User Studies

Although we know a great deal about which public library customers borrow what books, there is a good deal still to be learned about customer services and how those services relate to users. Motivations for using the public library, for example, still need more work like that of Marchant (1991). And how do we go about measuring equity of services? As part of a move toward more efficient allocation of resources, user service studies will continue in large numbers through the 1990s. There also is a need for specialized studies of youth services such as that of Lynch and Rockwood (1986).

Community Input and Involvement

Libraries, along with other public institutions, face a growing demand for community involvement, representation, and participation. "The library management team . . . must go into their communities and 'hustle'. They must actively seek out support . . . by listening to the needs and demands of the public" (McCabe & Kreissman, 1986, pp. 1-2). Discerning community needs will have to be done directly, through meetings, focus groups, and surveys (Sherman & Sanders, 1989, pp. 140-143).

Demand for Quality Customer Service

With the existence of competitive alternatives, public libraries will be pressured to deliver quality customer service. This demand includes the expectation that "librarians must lead us into this new and exciting world" of electronic database searching (Snyder, 1986; Sherman & Sanders, 1989, pp. 144-148).

Technological Innovation

Machine Searching

Helping customers deal with the electronic search environment calls for new kinds of instruction in library use and information searching (Oberman, 1991; Baker, Huston, & Pastine, 1991) and the creation of more hospitable social and intellectual settings for end-users (Miericke,

1991). Ultimately library practitioners will help design friendly search environments, including those utilizing "probabilistic 'best-match' weighting and ranking schemes derived from information retrieval research, . . . hypertext-style browsing . . . and heuristic . . . searching . . . [with] clues" (Larson, 1991, pp. 224-229).

Multimedia

Multimedia access platforms will become the principal form of individual access to electronic databases (Gates, 1991), especially desired by those who use libraries regularly as information gateways. The promise of multimedia is the ability to search a wide variety of databases, including those in different media, with one search routine (IBM, 1991, p. F2). The use of artificially intelligent 'agents' . . . to serve as personalized information services for users will accelerate the trend (Young, 1989, pp. 7-10).

Virtual Libraries

The potential of virtual libraries, a technology system that makes it possible to use a library without being inside a library building, which was fully articulated by scholar F. W. Lancaster (1982) more than a decade ago, is now being realized. Virtual libraries are now coming into their own. They may be free-standing or included with a branch or central library (Ghikas, 1989, pp. 123-124). The massive adoption of dial-in catalogs by public libraries marks a significant beginning. Public libraries already are mounting other customer information services and products on these catalogs.

Lancaster notes that virtual libraries have profound implications because librarianship is "perhaps the most institutionalized of all the professions" (Lancaster, 1982, p. 137). Virtual libraries challenge this institutional identity (Dowlin, 1986).

Demands for Currency

In a mature information age, time will become the new strategic frontier (Time, 1990). Public library customers increasingly will want this month's magazine, not one from two years ago. In response, the public library will organize just-in-time delivery of needed material using electronic mechanisms.

New Product Design and Evaluation

Through the next decade we will see many individual public libraries produce databases to export to other libraries online, on CD-ROM, through fax, or in standard paper formats (Szynaka & Cain, 1989;

Neff, 1991, p. 17). To reduce costs and protect their futurity, public libraries also will become more involved in new product testing (Boss & Casey, 1991).

Alternative Futures

As part of their strategic planning, individuals, organizations, and companies have begun to explore alternative futures for public libraries. The rate of technological change makes it imperative for individual institutions to conduct environmental scans, to assess strengths and weaknesses, and to consider alternative futures based on different causal scenarios. These behaviors suggest the need for sophisticated strategic planning.

DEVELOPING AN INSTITUTIONAL RESEARCH AGENDA

Research is a good tool to help public libraries achieve their strategic futures. Because of differences in their history, stages of development, and contexts, libraries are likely to have different research needs at any particular time.

As public library practitioners, SLPL administration and staff recognize that our institution is part of a larger library community but one with current needs and a history that is particularly our own. Our research strategy is built on this observation. We borrow whatever we can from wherever we can find it. The literature search, the calls to colleagues who may have had similar experiences, the glances outside the profession to see if other public sector institutions or private sector companies can furnish models for behavior all precede any thought of attempting to set up and undertake research. Our policy is to undertake research only when there seems no other way to find out what needs to be known.

The SLPL research experience over the past four years demonstrates how particular institutional needs translate into research concentrations. A listing of SLPL studies can be found in the Appendix. A summary of the research themes follows.

One group of studies has involved analysis of constituencies—to find out what users and potential users want, how they use the library, the depth of their support, and whether they will increase funding. Constituency studies form the basis for specific policy changes—and a grounding for institutional marketing. Constituency research helped SLPL win a tax campaign in 1988 and suggested priorities for how new funding should be used.

Creation of a revised policy for collections development was a second research area. A staff team undertook extensive collections assessments and gathered collections policy documents from around the country. The new collections development policy has had enormous impact, offering substantial guidance to institutional buying and weeding. This new policy has focused collecting and helped reduce the cost of storing materials.

Another group of studies demonstrates the library's interest in adding value to our collections by increasing access points. Publications on local and ethnic history, the art history collection, and an ongoing bibliographies program increase access to the library's rich holdings. Several of these publications also have earned incidental income and have served the more general purpose of enhancing institutional visibility. The collections studies have allowed critical development of our research and reference collections, which, with appropriate staffing, helps make the library a community knowledge center.

Two related study categories, technology and facilities, both involved capital investment and, therefore, the element of futurity discussed in a previous section of the paper. The high cost of capital investments has led to extensive study before expenditure is made. One study—a facilities needs assessment for all buildings in the system— cost more than $400,000. And staff spent many work-months developing criteria for the new DEC VAX to replace the old mainframe. The result of these studies has been effective expenditure of taxpayer funds.

Planning also occupied a great deal of time. Planning efforts involved developing the library's first formal master and strategic plans and the establishment of the library's first sustained fund raising program. Planning is at the core of modern library management, and, as Brooke Sheldon (1989) has suggested, no modern development program can do well without it. The library undertook inquiries to improve the quality of management and operations. These assessments resulted in the establishment of in-service training program for top-level and intermediate managers, the installation of a preventative maintenance program, and the movement of some incidental support services like lawn maintenance and snow removal from staff to contractors.

Two final observations about the studies. Over 30 percent of them involved a paid consultant as the principal or as a consulting author. In every case, the library was well-served by its consultants, most of whom were professionals from outside library science. This fact should not be misinterpreted; it reflects the strength of skills of librarians on staff and the range of knowledge specialties that a relatively large library system needs in making sound management decisions.

The second observation is a warning that the brief summary in this section should not be regarded as advocacy for institutional research only on the topics outlined. Every library needs to set its own research agenda. For the public library practitioner, research is a policy-making imperative. But research is not cheap, and it takes time. Research is never undertaken for fun or for show. Public library research should be executed when policy makers need information or answers that they can obtain in no other way.

BUILDING AN INFRASTRUCTURE FOR
PUBLIC LIBRARY RESEARCH

Because research is a policy-making imperative in American public libraries, there is a need to build its support infrastructure (McClure, 1989). Development of such an infrastructure, however, is a task with many dimensions (Rothman, 1980, passim).

To start, academy-based library researchers must learn to communicate with public library policy makers on some equal basis (McClure, 1991). This communication will have the most impact if accomplished as part of specific marketing mechanisms that reach into practitioners' work lives (Hevey, 1984).

As part of their communication with practitioners, scholar-researchers need to develop dissemination strategies that apply before, during, and at the conclusion of their research projects (Havard-Williams & Stewart, 1986, p. 33). That means announcing research in newsletters like *Library Hotline* and *Urban Libraries Exchange* (Lyman et al., 1982, pp. 46-52). It also means the need for more research-based articles in widely circulated library journals (Magrill, 1984).

Electronic networks provide a research-information distribution mechanism much easier to control. The University of Illinois PLATO system, for example, offers the opportunity for library school scholars and practitioners to work together to start an interactive library journal of the type that F. Wilfrid Lancaster suggested almost a decade ago (Lancaster, 1982, pp. 66-70).

Beyond electronic communication, there are conferences and conventions, which are a mainstay of communication for all professions—because they work. The better ones showcase talent and new ideas, especially those of older management professionals who tend to be more interested in research than younger practitioners (Lyman et al., 1982, pp. 13-24). Conferences also expand networks, a primary source of information for practitioners as they conduct a policy inquiry (Lyman et al., 1982, pp. 13, 46, 52).

Another benefit may be to reveal to public librarians that they already use research techniques in their daily work even though they do not regard themselves as interested in "scientific research" (Hill,

1986, pp. 746-749). The Allerton and the Data Processing conferences at the University of Illinois and the conferences on information technology at the University of Pittsburgh offer excellent examples.

Those most interested in widening interest in library science research among practitioners need to target library directors and upper-level public library managers for special attention. Such persons determine if institutional research will be conducted and how it will be resourced.

Library directors who already see research as a policy-making imperative have an important role to play as well. Within their own institutions, they can offer key staff financial support for travel to conventions and conferences where research is featured, schedule work so that staff have time to conduct research, hire consultants where needed, and purchase a sufficient body of materials to keep staff alerted to research developments in the library field (Camp, Anderson, & Mosby, 1989, pp. 9-14; Hewitt, 1991; Hoadley, 1991, pp. 184-188).

Although they will be helpful, the strategies I have suggested for building a public library research infrastructure will be insufficient if used alone. With so much research needed, there must be movement beyond exhortations. The latter include Lenox (1985), Farmer (1985, 1986), Varlejs (1987), and Swisher (1986).

Momentum for more public library research will require a broad-based and focused collaborative effort. Fortunately, the model for that collaboration already exists in the library profession. It is, of course, the Public Library Inquiry.

The Public Library Inquiry was inspired by a desire to modernize public library practices at the end of World War II. The strategy was collegial in tone and cooperative so far as research talents involved.

The Inquiry obtained a grant from the Carnegie Foundation and then set to its work. The Inquiry organizers gathered prestigious social science and humanities scholars and joined them with scholars and practitioners from inside the profession. Studies and publications poured out, enough to fill many volumes of books and journals. At the end of the Inquiry, the volume of research on public library policy and operations had increased exponentially (Berelson, 1949; Leigh, 1950; Bryan, 1952).

At the same time, questions that practitioners still most want to answer had been posed. Bernard Berelson (1949) in his volume, for example, suggested the need for more quantitative studies of library use and users, for practitioners to take a more active role in defining research needs, whether or not opinion makers used the public library, how the poorly educated could be induced to make greater use of the library, if the library had any impact on keeping students from dropping out of schools, the "social utility" of library services, and "unrecorded use" of the public library (i.e., noncirculation measures) (pp. 112-132).

I do not propose that we replicate the Public Library Inquiry. I do suggest that it remains the most profound, connected, sustained, and most focused attempt to conduct research *about* and *for* the American public library. For years the Inquiry focused attention on public library research. And for a decade during and after the Inquiry, it engaged public libraries in the research process.

Building on the model of the Public Library Inquiry has some real advantages. It builds on existent structures rather than attempting to create a wholly new "think tank"; its strategy is collaborative, a traditional way of doing business in the library profession; and it has the potential for inducing a significant body of practitioners to become stakeholders in research projects. (In St. Louis, the initiative associated with the Inquiry produced a number of studies, including Compton [1939], University of Denver [1945], and Bruns [1951].)

A new inquiry also could be designed to contain successful training and dissemination mechanisms and incentives for those who become part of the training network to start research on their own. And it could offer the opportunity to establish a mechanism for constructing bridges between researchers and library managers. Charles McClure (1989, pp. 292-293) maintains that this absent bridge has been the missing linchpin in the practitioner-academic researcher equation since Herbert Goldhor assumed a leadership role in promoting library science research more than three decades ago.

Reinventing the Public Library Inquiry for a new generation recognizes that a latent market already exists for applied research. It also recognizes that many public libraries currently conduct research, but that this research is not widely disseminated through the formal distribution mechanisms of the profession.

To quote Susan Beck (1987), who led an unsuccessful attempt to get practitioners to publish their studies:

> Internal projects on which we spend long hours can be enhanced by a written analysis of the processes and results of the project. In some cases reports are written for internal distribution, describing the processes used to solve specific problems. Such studies will often be useful to other librarians. We must communicate these results and conclusions with one another. (p. 3)

Unlike the unsuccessful publication that Beck attempted to compile, a new Public Library Inquiry does not require a consensus of the disinterested to make it happen. It allows those most interested in action research in public libraries to undertake research, to disseminate that work, and to promote the further development of support for research in a focused, collaborative way.

Oliver Wendell Holmes reminded us years ago that "the first step toward improvement is to look the facts in the face." The facts are these. Public libraries are not one thing but many, and there is an insufficiency of research on which to deal with their variant needs. Many public library practitioners are doing research, but their world of finding out and resource sharing is different from academic researchers. Most practitioner research is localistic in purpose. It goes without saying that many libraries do not do very much, if any, research.

This situation grows more critical in a fast-changing environment where the future is at best uncertain. St. Louis Public is one library that has developed a research imperative to deal with these uncertainties. We do not want to claim too much for our research and inquiry efforts, but they have met our policy-making and decision-making needs. The studies have helped make easier the development of strategic policies.

This paper ends where it began—by asserting that research is a public library policy-making imperative. It can help public library practitioners offer high-quality services to all constituencies while adapting to rapid changes and at the same time positioning institutions for the future.

Those of us at St. Louis Public Library who have undertaken our own institutional research hope that others who share our point of view will want to work with us to promote public library research. If we can generate a focused and collaborative research effort, the research work of a few can benefit many more. In the process, more of America's public libraries can gain the tools to deal strategically with the forces for change associated with information-age convergence and new competition.

ACKNOWLEDGMENTS

The author acknowledges the valuable research and reference assistance of Anne Watts, head of the Downtown Branch operation at SLPL's Central Library, in preparing this article. Thanks also to Professor Ron Powell, associate professor and chair of the Department of Library Science, School of Library and Information Science, University of Missouri, Columbia, MO, for furnishing me several bibliographic items and to colleagues Mary Mulroy, Dr. Leslie Edmonds, and David Smith for critiquing the paper at several stages of its development.

APPENDIX

Annotated Listing of
St. Louis Public Library Research Projects, 1987-1991

[Abernathy, Fred] (1991). *Public safety procedures for the St. Louis Public Library*. Development of a training and procedures manual for staff orientation and reference. Based upon contacts with many other libraries, consultation with attorneys, and a literature search.

[Abernathy, Fred] (1991). *Security plan for the St. Louis Public Library*. Plan developed after contact with many other institutions, a literature search, and consultation with attorneys. Resulted in rekeying and installation of electronic alarming systems in all library facilities.

[Abernathy, Fred; Piquet, Jeanette] (1990). *St. Louis Public Library disaster response guide*. Established priorities and procedures for institutional response to fires, floods, earthquakes, etc. Drew on disaster manuals from other cultural institutions, especially libraries and museums; conversations with disaster-preparedness officials; assessments of codes and hazards in relationship to libraries. Authorship paired a former policeman, now head of SLPL security, and a librarian.

Ackerman, Aric S.; Holman, Rodney G.; & the staff of Attitude Research Corporation (1990). *St. Louis Public Library. Coro Foundation market survey report*. An examination of knowledge of, use of, and support for SLPL in comparison with other major area cultural institutions with a structured sample telephone survey. Sample instrument developed in consultation with a professional survey research firm. Statistical reliability tests applied.

Alloway, Catherine; Bouchard, Celia; McDonald, Brenda; Smith, Lori (1991). Field-tested reference books: A survey of what has worked best. *Wilson Library Bulletin, 65*(January), pp. 26-31, 137-140. Purpose: To share knowledge about reference-book usefulness with other librarians. The second of two articles a year apart on the same subject by SLPL staff, assisted by other reference librarians.

By Design, Inc. (1991). *Architectural drawings and blueprints for the Julia Davis Branch Library*. Architectural and engineering bid and design specifications developed with heavy staff involvement.

Cohen, Aaron, and Associates (1990). *St. Louis Public Library Main Branch five-year building program*. (Croton-on-Hudson, NY, 1 March 1990). A master space plan for Central Library through 2010. Involved extensive statistical survey of current and future space needs based on linear-foot count of shelving needs and square-foot assessments of service and support needs. Devised formula estimates for space needs for 5 years and for 20 years.

Community Consultants, Inc. (1987). *Tracking poll results, 1, 2, ...* Assessment of potential voter support for a library tax referendum in order to establish weak and strong areas of support. A structured sample telephone survey of registered voters by census tract. Use of verifiable statistical methodologies, with rate of error assessed.

Edmonds, Leslie (1991). Can they really find it on their own? Children's use of public library catalogs. (Paper presented at the PLA Convention, San Diego, CA, 22 March 1991). Based on a literature review and Edmonds' ongoing research in this field.

Edmonds, Leslie (1991). Starting out right: The effectiveness of online catalogs in providing bibliographic access to youth. In Martin A. Siegel (Ed.), *Design and evaluation of computer/human interfaces: Issues for librarians and information scientists* (Papers presented at the 1988 Clinic on Library Applications of Data Processing, 17-19 April 1988) (pp. 139-161). Urbana-Champaign: University of Illinois Graduate School of Library and Information Science. Based on a literature review and author's continuing research in this field.

Edmonds, Leslie; Jacobsen, Frances F.; Sutton, Ellen (1991). Reference services to special groups. In Richard E. Bopp & Linda Smith (Eds.), *Reference and information services: An introduction*. Littleton, CO: Libraries Unlimited. Based on a literature review and the authors' continuing research in this field.

Edmonds, Leslie; Moore, Paula; Balcom, Kathleen Mehaffey (1990). The effectiveness of an online catalog: Determining how well students use the technology. *School Library Journal, 36*(October), pp. 28-32. Included in *Library lit 21: The best of 1990*. Based on a literature review and authors' continuing research in this field.

Franzwa, Gregory (forthcoming 1994). *The Lincoln highway: A history, gazetteer and guide*. (Vols. 1-4). Tucson, AZ: The Patrice Press and the St. Louis Public Library. Co-publication of an important reference work, which will involve extensive use of the library's collections. Publication will raise the visibility of the library and its collections. Work is under way by a well-known author and publisher.

[Gosebrink, Jean] (1988). *What's in the St. Louis Public Library cat-fiche and bibliographic database?* Printed users guide drawing on pre-announcement tests by staff and patrons.

[Gosebrink, Jean] (Comp.) (1989). *St. Louis Public Library board of directors orientation manual*. Revised for each new board member, a loose-leaf notebook compilation of all statutes and policies affecting SLPL operations along with minutes of recent meetings and ALA canons and guidelines.

[Gosebrink, Jean E. Meah] (Comp.) (1991). *St. Louis: An annotated bibliography on the city & its area*. Compilation and annotation of the first significant bibliographic treatment of St. Louis history and culture in over a decade, stressing recently published works. Methodology: Included review and annotation of all recent scholarly and popular work on the community's history and culture.

[Holobeck, Noel] (1991). *The German-American heritage of St. Louis: A guide*. The inaugural publication of the SLPL Local Area Studies Center intended to create knowledge of the library's local history and genealogy collections and its status as the official repository of the archives of the German-American Society of St. Louis. The publication described fifty historical buildings and sites and included an auto tour map of the locations.

[Holt, Glen E.] (1987). *St. Louis Public Library background fact book*. Development and compilation of documents used by all library spokespersons throughout the 1987-1988 tax campaign.

[Holt, Glen E.] (1988). *St. Louis Public Library master plan. Goals and objectives for the library, 1989-1994*. Development of the institution's first master plan, based on a literature review, unit assessments, and consultations with library and other cultural institution directors.

Holt, Glen E. (1990). Redefining the library's place. (Paper presented at the session, *The reality of changing and changed environments*, ALA Annual Convention, Chicago, IL, 26 June 1990). Presentation of a rationale for and the results of SLPL's use of off-site computers, vans, and programs to enhance library service for niche markets in St. Louis.

[Holt, Glen E.] (1991). *A community information system for the City of St. Louis by several developmental partners and the St. Louis Public Library.* A rationale and plan for a community information system. Document used to publicize development and attract donors. Document created after an extensive review of the literature on various urban information systems. Resulted in active partnerships with information companies.

[Holt, Glen E.; Junz, A.] (1989). *Documents organizing the Foundation for the benefit of the St. Louis Public Library.* (St. Louis, Adopted by the Board of Directors of the St. Louis Public Library Foundation, 11 September 1989). Development of a rationale, an organizing structure, and all documents to start a library foundation and a development program.

[Holt, Glen E.; Smith, David] (1989). *St. Louis Public Library strategic plan.* Revised and updated in 1990 and 1991, this document guides the development of all policies and budgeting.

[Jinks, Paul, et al.] (1988). *Salary market study.* (Semi-annual). Analysis of all relevant reports on the salaries of all categories of library, government, and cultural institution workers. Mathematical formulae, with adjustments gradually refined, integrating national statistics from ALA, PLA, and SLA with those for local and regional markets. Results in accurate picture of "salary market" for all staff. Used to determine entry and range levels of all salary categories.

[Jinks, Paul] (1989). *A pay-for-performance plan for the St. Louis Public Library.* Revised in 1990 and implemented in 1991. An assessment of library, cultural institution, and corporate literature to propose a plan which would work at SLPL.

[Jinks, Paul] (1989). *Position evaluation plan for the St. Louis Public Library.* A study that preceded the writing of new job descriptions.

[Jinks, Paul] (1990). *Personnel policies.* Development of up-to-date, legal personnel policies reflecting current operations at SLPL.

[Junz, Al] (1988). *A proposal for a St. Louis Public Library business information center at the St. Louis Centre.* A true feasibility study considering the move of a library business, science, and technology unit to the most significant downtown shopping center. Modeled on retail location studies. Concept rejected after costs and benefits assessed.

Koch & Associates, Inc. (1988). *Architectural drawings and blueprints for an elevator for the handicapped.* Architectural and engineering bid and design specifications with heavy staff involvement.

Koch & Associates, Inc. (1991). *Feasibility study regarding the financial feasibility of relocating the technical services department to Compton Branch Library.* Analysis of capital costs and changes in operating costs from an architectural and engineering perspective.

Marketing Edge, Inc., The (1990). *The Julia Davis [Branch] Library focus group report.* Structured focus groups with neighborhood citizens to explore their perceptions of needed services and interior design of a new branch library. Interviews resulted in several significant changes to the interior and exterior plans for a new branch library.

Mulroy, Mary; with Kafron, Charles (1990). *Branch services study.* An analysis of branch services using statistical analysis of transaction-load and census-tract statistics. Statistical reliability tests applied. Quantitative findings expressed in tables, maps, and bar graphs. Computer mapping used in presentation of the work.

Numerof & Associates, Inc. (1989). *Managing for organizational effectiveness.* Development of a program to improve the quality of middle-level library management by an industrial psychologist working with managers to assess training needs. Resulted in a 43-hour management training seminar for middle managers, including all librarians.

Numerof & Associates, Inc. (1990). *Continuing education development [for St. Louis Public Library Managers].* Development of a program to improve the quality of upper-level library management by an industrial psychologist working with managers to assess training needs. Resulted in nearly 100 hours of formal in-service, seminar discussion training for upper-level managers.

Peters, Frank (1992). *Historical Midwest buildings: The Piaget photographs in the Library of Congress.* (St. Louis: The Patrice Press and the St. Louis Public Library, forthcoming 1992). Co-publication of an important reference work revealing the architectural heritage of the Midwest and the St. Louis region. Publication will raise the visibility of the library and its midwestern collections. Project nearly completed. Authorship by a Pulitzer Prize-winning journalist and respected St. Louis-area author.

[Peterson, Kim] (1991). *Interlibrary loan study.* Used OCLC statistics to assess net-lending demands and to predict impact of changes made in Missouri State Library computerized access system. Resulted in policy decisions regarding ILL charges.

Porter, E. F., Jr. (1990). *Harland Bartholomew.* (Bibliography by Jean Gosebrink). St. Louis: St. Louis Public Library and the Landmarks Association of St. Louis, Inc. An exhibition catalog and guide to the library's holdings on St. Louisan Harland Bartholomew, an early leader in the city planning movement in the United States.

Price Waterhouse, St. Louis Office (1989). *Saint Louis Public Library. Management review of finance office* (St. Louis, 11 January 1989). Three certified public accountants conducted detailed procedural analysis of the library's financial practices, compared SLPL with norms for public sector institutions, and made wide-ranging recommendations for changes in policies and procedures.

Ross & Baruzzini, Inc. Engineers-Architects; Koch & Associates, Architects (1988). *St. Louis Public Library facilities needs assessment.* (2 vols.). A detailed facilities analysis and inventory that would guide all future rehabilitation and construction work on every building in the SLPL system, including fire protection and security requirements. Involved on-site analysis by certified and licensed construction engineers, engineering specialists, and architects.

Schlafly, Thomas (1991). Winning a tax election. (Paper presented at the session, *Funding fun: How to bait the money trap,* ALTA Education of Trustees Session, ALA Convention, Atlanta, GA, 30 June 1991). Summarized organization and methodology for winning a tax campaign. Schlafly is a regional vice-president of ALTA and twice president of the SLPL Board of Directors.

SLPL (1988). *Manual for using the St. Louis Public Library automated system.* A 55-page publication for staff to ready them to explain and demonstrate all electronic catalog functions and procedures. Drew on pre-announcement tests and product literature.

SLPL (1990). *Reference policy of the St. Louis Public Library.* Staff contacted many other libraries about reference policy, consulted with attorneys, and did literature search.

SLPL (1990-1991). *Walk-in and phone-in survey of Central Library.* (Quarterly). Regular surveys to determine the residential zip codes of Central Library users. Part of a long-term study connected with possibilities of reciprocal usage with other library systems.

SLPL (1991). *Collection development policy of the St. Louis Public Library.* A staff training and reference manual including a conspectus, definition of all collections, policies, and responsibilities involved in selection and weeding. Involved written analysis and descriptions of all collections, examination of literature on collections development and the collections development policies of many public and academic libraries.

SLPL (Mary Mulroy, Team Leader) (1990). *Building program for the Julia Davis Library.* A detailed building program that formed the basis of an RFP for an architect and a guide to design a new branch library.

SLPL, Technical Services (1991). *Missouri union list of serials project (MULSP).* (Annual since 1976). Compilation and production of the Missouri union list of serials under contract with the Missouri State Library. Publication issued electronically and in paper based on bibliographic compilation, updating, and cross-checking.

SLPL, Technical Services (1991). *Monograph acquisitions procedures manual.* Review of training manuals from other libraries and literature to create a staff training and reference guide.

SLPL, Technical Services (1991). *MULSP bibliographic record manual.* Designed to establish continuity and efficiency of record-inputs from entry to entry and from year to year.

SLPL, Technical Services (1991). *Serials acquisitions procedures manual.* Review of training manuals from other libraries and literature to create a staff training and reference guide.

[Smith, David] (1990). *RFP specifications for development of a computer main frame for St. Louis Public Library.* A multimonth assessment of future SLPL computer needs, the computing capacity of various machines, along with capital and operating expenses. Involved an extensive literature review, quantitative analysis of current and future needs, and cost analysis.

[Smith, David] (1991). *Literacy hotline software.* (Copyrighted and Marketed, 1991). Product developed under an LSCA grant issued so that other potential library users may have access to a neat software package.

Smith, David (1991). Planning for library automation obsolescence. (Paper presented at the session, *Weeding your terminals: Understanding and planning for library automation obsolescence,* PLA Convention, San Diego, CA, 21 March 1991). Analysis of rationale and intellectual and policy issues involved in single library-developed OPACs based on the SLPL experience.

[Smith, David] (1991). *St. Louis Public Library strategic plan update, 1990-1995.* Updated annually, this document serves to measure progress against planning.

Southwestern Bell Telephone Company (1991). *Assessment of telephone needs of Central Library.* Study to bring SLPL a modern, flexible communications system capable of sophisticated voice and data transfer. Hired a telephone consultant who helped staff specify needs, then allowed SWB's free consultant service to develop options for solving institutional problems. Resulted in a contract with SWB to remove SLPL from the telephone business in lieu of a digitized Plexar I System using Bell's Chestnut Street switching facility as the library's out-of-house PBX.

Telephone Contact Inc. (January-March 1988). *Library campaign telephone survey results, 1, 2, ...* Same purpose and methodology as in the previously cited study by Community Consultants, Inc. (1987).

[Tillinger, Elaine] (1992). *Dictionary of St. Louis artists.* A three-year project to compile an electronic dictionary of artists who worked in St. Louis between 1764 and 1950. Available as a reference tool in art history with plans for electronic and paper publication. Involved extensive primary and secondary research.

[Wandel, David] (1991). *Job descriptions of the St. Louis Public Library.* Revision of all SLPL descriptions to comply with all federal and state statutes and making them reflect changed (and changing) work conditions. The author, with more than fifteen years of human resources and operations managements in large hospitals and as a consultant to other institutions, researched and rewrote each policy. These were checked and rewritten by an operations consultant and by the library's attorneys.

[Wandel, David; Washington, Debra] (1990). *Staff training plan for St. Louis Public Library.* Development of a comprehensive training plan for all categories of SLPL staff. Established an inventory of training needs with recommendations on most effective training to be used.

Watts, Anne; Kofron, Charles P.; CPK Consulting Services (1990). *St. Louis Public Library business users survey.* Assessment of business information and library needs through a structured mail survey. A five-page survey instrument was mailed to 2,800 businesses in St. Louis, geo-coded by zip code. Statistical reliability tests applied. Survey formed the basis for major policy shifts and the development of a business, science, and technology unit.

REFERENCES

Altman, E., & Brown, S. (1991). What makes a librarian excellent? The view from Phoenix. *Public Libraries, 30*(4), 208-217.

Baker, B.; Huston, M. M.; & Pastine, M. (1991). Making connections: Teaching information retrieval. *Library Trends, 39*(3), 210-222.

Ballard, T. H. (1990). The unfulfilled promise of resource sharing. *American Libraries, 21*(10), 990-993.

Barker, J. (1991, June 10). Paradigms—Assessing the future. Keynote Address Part I, Annual Convention of the Special Libraries Association, San Antonio, TX.

Beach, C. (1989). The public library as provider of library services to educational institutions. In P. Woodrum (Ed.), Managing public libraries in the 21st century [Special issue]. *Journal of Library Administration, 11*(1/2), 173-187.

Beck, S. J. (1987). Guest editorial: Sharing ideas through research publications. *New Jersey Libraries, 20*(1), 1-4.

Bender, D. R. (1991). Twelve years of change: Looking back . . . and ahead. *SpeciaList, 14*(September), 8.

Berelson, B. (1949). *The public's library; A report of the Public Library Inquiry.* New York: Columbia University.

Berman, J. J. (1990). Public access to electronic public information. In J. A. Nelson (Ed.), *Gateways to comprehensive state information policy* (pp. 35-37). Lexington, KY: Published by the Chief Officers of State Library Agencies through the Council of State Governments.

Biggs, M. (1991). The scholarly vocation and library science. In I. P. Godden (Ed.), *Advances in librarianship* (Vol. 15, pp. 29-75). San Diego, CA: Academic Press.

Blegen, J. (1990). Beyond access: Implications of the information age for the public library. In V. L. P. Blake & R. Tjoumas (Eds.), *Information literacies for the twenty-first century* (A national conference held at Queens College Graduate School of Library and Information Studies, October 1988) (pp. 457-466). Boston: G. K. Hall.

Blodgett, T. (1986). The city in 2000 A.D.: A microcosm of American democracy. *Public Library Quarterly, 7*(3/4), 9-25.

Bolman, L. G., & Deal, T. E. (1991). *Reframing organizations: Artistry, choice and leadership.* San Francisco, CA: Jossey-Bass.

Boss, R. W., & Casey, M. H. (1991). Operating systems for automated library systems. *Library Technology Reports, 27*(2), 123-210.

Bruns, L. G. (1951). A survey of the St. Louis Public Library. Unpublished master's thesis, Rosary College, Riverforest, IL.

Bryan, A. I. (1952). *The public librarian; A report of the Public Library Inquiry.* New York: Columbia University.

Camp, J. A.; Anderson, D. G.; & Mosby, A. P. (1989). In the same boat together: Creating an environment for research and publication. In J. C. Fennell (Ed.), *Building on the first century* (Proceedings of the Fifth National Conference of the Association of College and Research Libraries, Cincinnati, OH, 5-8 April 1989) (pp. 9-14). Chicago: American Library Association, Association of College and Research Libraries.

Cargill, J., & Webb, G. M. (1988). *Managing libraries in transition.* Phoenix, AZ: Oryx Press.

Cetron, M., & Davies, O. (1990). Trends shaping the world. *The Futurist, 24*(5), 11-27.

Childers, T. (1984). Will the cycle be unbroken? Research and schools of library and information studies. *Library Trends, 32*(4), 521-535.

Compton, C. H. (1939). *The St. Louis Public Library today and tomorrow: A survey.* St. Louis, MO: St. Louis Public Library.

Converse, W. R. (1984). Research: What we need, and what we get. *Canadian Library Journal, 41*(5), 235-241.

Corbin, R. A. (1991). The development of the national research and education network. *Information Technology and Libraries, 10*(3), 212-220.

Croneberger, R. B. (1989). External influences on public library management in the 21st century. In P. Woodrum (Ed.), Managing public libraries in the 21st century [Special issue]. *Journal of Library Administration, 11*(1/2), 209-220.

D'Elia, G., with Rodger, E. J. (1991). *Free Library of Philadelphia patron survey: Final report.* Philadelphia, PA: Free Library of Philadelphia.

Dealers Return, The. (1991, September 16). *Time*, pp. 46-47.

Dowlin, K. (1986). The knowledge center. *Public Library Quarterly*, 7(3/4), 5-7.

Dowlin, K. (1991). The neographic library: An essay. A thirty-year perspective on public libraries, a work in progress. Typescript.

Drucker, P. F. (1988). The coming of the new organization. *Harvard Business Review*, 66(1), 45-53.

Enoch Pratt Free Library. (1989). *A plan for the 1990's.* Baltimore, MD: Enoch Pratt Free Library.

Epstein, H. (1989). Technological trends in information services to the 21st century. In M. M. Aman & D. J. Sager (Eds.), *Trends in urban library management: Proceedings of the Urban Library Management Institute held in October 1988 at the University of Wisconsin-Milwaukee.* Metuchen, NJ: Scarecrow Press.

Farmer, L. S. J. (1985). Locating research. *Top of the News*, 41(4), 397-398.

Farmer, L. S. J. (1986). Searching the solutions: Using research findings to improve library service to children and young adults. *Top of the News*, 43(1), 113-116.

Franks, M. (1991). Seattle Public Library, Research for Beacon Hill Branch. In *Seattle Public Library. Local Government Information Center. Recent Additions. New Local Documents.* (July), 7.

Freeman, M. S. (1985). 'The simplicity of his pragmatism': Librarians and research. *Library Journal*, 110(9), 27-29.

Furthering the vision: Three youth services specialists respond. (1989). *School Library Journal*, 35(14), 33-38.

Futas, E., & Zipkowitz, F. (1991). The faculty vanishes. *Library Journal*, 116(14), 148-152.

Gallagher, J. (1991, October 16). The 'dream' eludes young American families. *St. Louis Post-Dispatch*, 1F, 8F.

Garfield, E. (1988). Information scientists and the transformation of society. *Bulletin of the American Society for Information Science*, 14(5), 38-40.

Gates, W. H. (1991). Personal computing in the information age. (Forthcoming in the 1992 *Yearbook of science and the future*). Typescript.

Ghikas, M. W. (1989). Collection management for the 21st century. In P. Woodrum (Ed.), Managing public libraries in the 21st century [Special issue]. *Journal of Library Administration*, 11(1/2), 123-124.

Gilovich, T. (1991). *How we know what isn't so: The fallibility of human reason in everyday life.* New York: Free Press.

Goldstein, M. (1990). Year 2000. *Information services and use*, 10(6), 333-340.

Gunde, M. G. (1991). What every librarian should know about the Americans with Disabilities Act. *American Libraries*, 22(8), 806-809.

Havard-Williams, P., & Stewart, L. (1986). Problems of disseminating research information. In N. Tudor-Silovic & I. Mihel (Eds.), *Information research: Research methods in library and information science* (Proceedings of the International Seminar on Information Research, Dubrovnik, Yugoslavia, 19-24 May 1986) (pp. 27-42). London: Taylor Graham.

Hevey, D. (1984). Research dissemination: Sales pitch or public relations. *ESRC Newsletter*, 51(March 1984), 30.

Hewitt, J. A. (1991). The role of the library administrator in improving LIS research. In C. R. McClure & P. Hernon (Eds.), *Library and information science research: Perspectives and strategies for improvement* (pp. 163-178). Norwood, NJ: Ablex.

Hill, M. W. (1986). Involvement in research and development. In N. Tudor-Silovic & I. Mihel (Eds.), *Information research: Research methods in library and information science* (Proceedings of the International Seminar on Information Research, Dubrovnik, Yugoslavia, 19-24 May 1986) (pp. 43-53). London: Taylor Graham.

Hoadley, I. B. (1991). The role of practicing LIS professionals. In C. R. McClure & P. Hernon (Eds.), *Library and information science research: Perspectives and strategies for improvement* (pp. 179-188). Norwood, NJ: Ablex.

Holdings of 16 Philadelphia-area libraries to be added to OCLC Database. (1991). *OCLC Newsletter, 189*(January-February), 8.

IBM. (1991). *IBM Personal System/2. IBM Multimedia Solutions.* White Plains, NY: International Business Machines.

Information technology transforms the corporation. (1991). [Special issue]. *Planning Review, 19*(3).

Kidder, R. M. (1987). *An agenda for the 21st century.* Cambridge, MA: MIT Press.

Kuhn, T. (1962). *The structure of scientific revolutions.* Chicago: University of Chicago Press.

Lancaster, F. W. (1982). *Libraries and librarians in an age of electronics.* Arlington, VA: Information Resources Press.

Larson, R. R. (1991). Between Scylla and Charybdis: Subject searching in the online catalog. In I. P. Godden (Ed.), *Advances in librarianship* (Vol. 15, pp. 175-236). San Diego, CA: Academic Press.

LaRue, J., & LaRue, S. (1991). Is anybody home? Home schooling and the library. *Wilson Library Bulletin, 66*(1), 32-37, 136-137.

Leigh, R. D. (1950). *The public library in the United States; The general report of the Public Library Inquiry.* New York: Columbia University.

Lenox, M. F. (1985). The importance of using research in decision making. *Top of the News, 41*(3), 301-302.

Louv, R. (1990). *Childhood's future.* Boston: Houghton Mifflin.

Lyman, P.; Slater, M.; & Walker, R. (1982). *Research and the practitioner: Dissemination of research results within the library-information profession.* London: Aslib Occasional Publication No. 27.

Lynch, C. K., & Rockwood, P. E. (1986). Marketing strategy for children's services. *Public Library Quarterly, 7*(3/4), 27-40.

Magrill, R. M. (1984). Publishing of research in librarianship. *Library Trends, 32*(4), 557-577.

Malinconico, S. M. (1989). Librarians in an age of technology. *Library Administration & Management, 3*(3), 142-144.

Marchant, M. P. (1991). Motivators and user characteristics: Effect on service. *Public Libraries, 30*(4), 218-225.

Marchant, M. P., & England, M. M. (1989). Future trends in public library administration. In P. Woodrum (Ed.), Managing public libraries in the 21st century [Special issue]. *Journal of Library Administration, 11*(1/2), 1-26.

Mason, M. G. (1985). The future of the public library. *Library Journal, 110*(14), 136-139.

Mason, M. G. (1991). *Large urban libraries: Their roles, responsibilities and contributions. A study prepared for the Urban Libraries Council by Marilyn Gell Mason.* State College, PA: Urban Libraries Council.

McCabe, G. R., & Kreissman, B. (1986). *Advances in library administration and organization* (Vol. 6). Greenwich, CT: JAI Press.

McClure, C. R. (1989). Increasing the usefulness of research for library managers: Propositions, issues and strategies. *Library Trends, 38*(2), 280-294.

McClure, C. R. (1991). Communicating applied library/information science research to decision makers: Some methodological considerations. In C. R. McClure & P. Hernon (Eds.), *Library and information science research: Perspectives and strategies for improvement* (pp. 253-266). Norwood, NJ: Ablex.

McClure, C. R., & Bishop, A. P. (1989). The status of research in library/information science: Guarded optimism. *College and Research Libraries, 50*(2), 127-143.

McClure, C. R.; Bishop, A.; Doty, P.; & Rosenbaum, H. (1990). Realizing the promise of NREN: Social and behavioral considerations—A status report on a study in progress. In C. A. Parkhurst (Ed.), *Library perspectives on NREN: The national research and education network* (pp. 23-32). Chicago: Library and Information Technology Association.

Miericke, S. (1991). Creating hospitable environments for technologically naive users: Y'all come back now, hear! *Library Trends, 39*(3), 327-334.

Milwaukee Public Library. (1987). *Affirmative action program. 1987 plan.* Milwaukee, WI: Milwaukee Public Library.

Naisbitt, J., & Aburdene, P. (1990). *Megatrends 2000: Ten new directions for the 1990's.* New York: Morrow.

Neff, R. K. (1991). The library of the future. *MultiMedia Solutions, 5*(2), 16, 17.

Nitecki, D. A. (1983). Competencies required of public service librarians to use new technologies. In L. C. Smith (Ed.), *Professional competencies—Technology and the librarian* (Papers presented at the 1983 Clinic on Library Applications of Data Processing, 24-26 April 1983) (pp. 43-57). Urbana-Champaign: University of Illinois, Graduate School of Library and Information Science.

O'Brien, P. M. (1989). Quality leadership for the 21st century. In P. Woodrum (Ed.), Managing public libraries in the 21st century [Special issue]. *Journal of Library Administration, 11*(1/2), 27-34.

Oberman, C. (1991). Avoiding the cereal syndrome, Or critical thinking in the electronic environment. *Library Trends, 39*(3), 189-202.

OCLC—Online Computer Library Center. (1988). *The future of the public library: Conference proceedings.* Dublin, OH: OCLC.

OCLC—Online Computer Library Center. (1990). *Interlibrary loan discussion panel: Final report.* Dublin, OH: OCLC.

Panz, R. (1989). Library services to special population groups in the 21st century. In P. Woodrum (Ed.), Managing public libraries in the 21st century [Special issue]. *Journal of Library Administration, 11*(1/2), 151-171.

Patterson, G. A. (1991, August 29). Building 'em better: Two GM auto plants illustrate major role of workers' attitudes. *The Wall Street Journal,* pp. A-1, A-5.

Penniman, W. D. (1991a, September 6). Remarks at a meeting of the St. Louis Research Library Directors Group. Transcript of meeting notes.

Penniman, W. D. (1991b, September 5). Stretching funding dollars for libraries. Speech given at Washington University, St. Louis, MO. Typescript.

Perry, B. J. (1986). Research policy formulation: Constraints and challenges. In N. Tudor-Silovic & I. Mihel (Eds.), *Information research: Research methods in library and information science* (Proceedings of the International Seminar on Information Research, Dubrovnik, Yugoslavia, 19-24 May 1986) (pp. 6-17). London: Taylor Graham.

Podolsky, A. (1991). *Public libraries in 50 states and the District of Columbia, 1989.* Washington, DC: U. S. Department of Education. Office of Educational Research and Improvement, National Center for Education Statistics.

Price, D. de S. (1980). Happiness is a warm librarian. In F. W. Lancaster, (Ed.), The role of the library in an electronic society (Papers presented at the 1979 Clinic on Library Applications on Data Processing, 22-25 April 1979) (pp. 3-15). Urbana-Champaign: University of Illinois, Graduate School of Library Science.

Prottas, J. M. (1981). The cost of free services: Organizational impediments to access to public services. *Public Administration Review, 41*(5), 526-534.

Public Library Association, Public Library Data Service. (1991). *Statistical Report '91.* Chicago: Public Library Association.

Research Alert Editors. (1991). *Future vision: The 189 most important trends for the 1990s.* Naperville, IL: Sourcebooks Trade.

Robinson, C. W. (1989). Free or fee based library in the year 2000. In P. Woodrum (Ed.), Managing public libraries in the 21st century [Special issue]. *Journal of Library Administration, 11*(1/2), 111-118.

Rothman, J. (1980). *Using research in organizations. A guide to successful application* (Vol. 101). Beverly Hills, CA: Sage Library of Social Research.

Sager, D. J. (1981). Partnership and competition in the public and private sectors. In A. Kent & T. J. Galvin (Eds.), *Information technology: Critical choices for library decision-makers* (Proceedings of a conference held in Pittsburgh, November 1981) (pp. 303-312). New York: Marcel Dekker.

Sager, D. J. (Ed.). (1991). Should public libraries be compensated for loaning materials to nonresidents, and if so, by whom? *Public Libraries, 30*(4), 201-207.

Schlachter, G. (1989). Research, one step at a time. *RQ, 28*(3), 293-294.

Sheldon, B. E. (1989). Strategic planning for public library services in the 21st century. In P. Woodrum (Ed.), Managing public libraries in the 21st century [Special issue]. *Journal of Library Administration, 11*(1/2), 199-208.

Sherman, M., & Sanders, J. (1989). Community involvement and support of the public library in the 21st century. In P. Woodrum (Ed.), Managing public libraries in the 21st century [Special issue]. *Journal of Library Administration, 11*(1/2), 137-150.

Sherrill, L. L. (Ed.). (1970). *Library service to the unserved* (Papers presented at a library conference held at the University of Wisconsin-Milwaukee, School of Library and Information Science, 16-18 November 1967). New York: Bowker Library and Information Science Studies No. 2.

Siegel, M. A. (Ed.). (1991). *Design and evaluation of computer/human interfaces: Issues for librarians and information scientists* (Papers presented at the 1988 Clinic on Library Applications of Data Processing, 17-19 April 1988). Urbana-Champaign: University of Illinois Graduate School of Library and Information Science.

Smith, L. C. (1991). From data processing to knowledge engineering: The impact of automation on public services. In M. A. Siegel (Ed.), *Design and evaluation of computer/human interfaces: Issues for librarians and information scientists* (Papers presented at the 1988 Clinic on Library Applications of Data Processing, 17-19 April 1988) (pp. 3-25). Urbana-Champaign: University of Illinois Graduate School of Library and Information Science.

Smulyan, M. H. (1989). *Recommendations for a strategic plan for the San Francisco Public Library, 1989-1995. Part I: Moving into the 21st century; Part II: Background information.* (ERIC Document Reproduction Service No. ED 311 915)

Snyder, D. P., & Edwards, G. (1991, July 1). America in the 1990's: An economy in transition, a society under stress. Paper delivered at the ALA Convention, Atlanta, GA. Typescript.

Snyder, H. (1986). Quiescence, query, quandary, quietus: Public services in the library of the future. *College and Research Libraries, 47*(6), 564-568.

Sorensen, C. (1989). Theme parks and time machines. In P. Vergo (Ed.), *The new museology* (pp. 60-73). London: Reaktion Books.

St. Louis Public Library Staff [Principal author Paul Jinks]. (1990). *Pay-for-performance study for the St. Louis Public Library.* St. Louis, MO: SLPL. Typescript.

Stieg, M. F. (1991). The closing of library schools: Darwinism at the university. *Library Quarterly, 61*(3), 266-272.

Summers, F. W. (1989). A vision of librarianship. *School Library Journal, 35*(14), 25-30.

Sunnydale, CA, City of. (1990). *Library sub-element, City of Sunnydale general plan.* Sunnydale, CA: City of Sunnydale.

Swigger, K. (1985). Institutional affiliations of authors of research articles. *Journal of Education for Library and Information Science, 26*(2), 105-109.

Swisher, R. (1986). Using research. *Top of the News, 42*(2), 175-177.

Swisher, R., & McClure, C. R. (1984). *Research for decision making: Methods for librarians.* Chicago: American Library Association.

Szynaka, E. M., & Cain, A. H. (1989). Local databases: The future of public libraries. In P. Woodrum (Ed.), Managing public libraries in the 21st century [Special issue]. *Journal of Library Administration, 11*(1/2), 189-198.

Thornburg, L. (1991). What's wrong with Workforce 2000? *HR Magazine on Human Resource Management, 36*(8), 39-42.

Time: The new strategic frontier. (1990). *Planning Review, 18*(6), 4-7, 46-48.

Toffler, A. (1990). *Power shift: Knowledge, wealth, and violence at the edge of the 21st century.* New York: Bantam.

Townley, C. T. (1989). Reluctant cooperation: Improving academic and large public library participation in multitype networks. In J. C. Fennell (Ed.), *Building on the first century* (Proceedings of the fifth national conference of the Association of College and Research Libraries, Cincinnati, OH, 5-8 April 1989) (pp. 98-102). Chicago: American Library Association, Association of College and Research Libraries.

Trezza, A. F. (1989). Sources of funding for public libraries. In P. Woodrum (Ed.), Managing public libraries in the 21st century [Special issue]. *Journal of Library Administration, 11*(1/2), 67-80.

U. S. Department of Education. Office of Educational Research and Improvement. (1987). *Rethinking the library in the information age: Issues in library research; Proposals for the 1990s* (Vol. II). Washington, DC: U. S. Department of Education, Office of Educational Research and Improvement.

United Way Strategic Institute. (1988). *Nine forces reshaping America.* Bethesda, MD: World Future Society.

United Way Strategic Institute. (1990). Nine forces reshaping America. *The Futurist, 24*(4), 9-16.

University of Denver, National Opinion Research Center. (1945). *Do people use their public library?* (Report prepared especially for St. Louis Public Library, St. Louis, Missouri. Based on a survey made for the American Library Association and seventeen cooperating city libraries). Denver, CO: NORC.

Van House, N. A. (1991). Assessing the quantity, quality, and impact of LIS research. In C. R. McClure & P. Hernon (Eds.), *Library and information science research: Perspectives and strategies for improvement* (pp. 85-100). Norwood, NJ: Ablex.

Van House, N.; Lynch, M. J.; McClure, C. R.; Zweizig, D. L; & Rodger, E. J. (1987). *Output measures for public libraries: A manual of standardized procedures.* Chicago: American Library Association.

Vanderkolk, B. S., & Young, A. A. (1991). *The work and family revolution: How companies can keep employees happy and business profitable.* New York: Facts on File.

Varlejs, J. (1987). Beyond 'Nostalgia and Mythology': A research agenda for public library young adult services. *Top of the News, 43*(4), 406-409.

Waterman, R. H. (1987). *The renewal factor: How the best get and keep the competitive edge.* New York: Bantam.

Watson, P. D. (1985). Production of scholarly articles by academic librarians and library school faculty. *College and Research Libraries, 46*(4), 334-342.

Webster, D. E. (1987). The impact of library technology on management. In D. C. Genaway (Ed.), *Proceedings of the Conference on Integrated Online Systems* (pp. 173-189). Canfield, OH: Genaway & Associates.

Wedgeworth, R. (1991, September 18). Opening banquet address. Paper presented at the annual conference of the Missouri Library Association, St. Louis, MO.

Weiss, M. J. (1988). *The clustering of America.* New York: Harper & Row.

Weiss, M. J. (1989). Clustered America: The communities we serve. *Public Libraries, 28*(3), 161-165.

Westin, A. F., & Finger, A. L. (1991). *Using the public library in the computer age: Present patterns, future possibilities: A national public opinion survey report by the Reference Point Foundation, in cooperation with the American Library Association.* Chicago: American Library Association.

Whitlatch, J. B. (1991). Automation and job satisfaction among reference librarians. *Computers in Libraries, 11*(8), 32-34.

Working from home. (1991, August). *St. Louis Commerce,* pp. 19-20.

Wright, P. (1989). The quality of visitors' experiences in art museums. In P. Vergo (Ed.), *The new museology* (pp. 119-148). London: Reaktion Books.

Wurman, R. S. (1989). *Information anxiety.* New York: Doubleday.

Wysocki, B., Jr. (1991, August 28). Overseas calling: American firms send office work abroad to use cheaper labor. *The Wall Street Journal,* pp. A-1, A-4.

Yankelovich, D. (1981). *New rules: Searching for self-fulfillment in a world turned upside down.* New York: Bantam Books.

Young, P. H. (1989). Library research in the future: A prognostication. *College and Research Libraries News, 50*(1), 7-10.

Zuboff, S. (1985). Technologies that informate: Implications for human resource management in the computerized industrial workplace. In R. E. Walton & P. R. Lawrence (Eds.), *HRM, trends and challenges* (pp. 103-139). Boston: Harvard Business School Press.

Zuboff, S. (1988). *In the age of the smart machine: The future of work and power.* New York: Basic Books.

KEITH CURRY LANCE

Director
Library Research Service
State Library and Adult Education Office
Colorado Department of Education
Denver, Colorado

KATY SHERLOCK

(Former) Assistant Director
Library Research Center
Graduate School of Library and Information Science
University of Illinois at Urbana-Champaign

Use of Statistics in Management Decisions

ABSTRACT

In using statistics in decision making, library managers can draw on five types of available data: library statistics, library salaries, employment outlook statistics, indexes of inflation and living costs, and demographic and economic data. In applying these data to management decisions, library managers can also utilize five strategies: taking the user's point of view, comparing libraries, tracking trends and making projections, indexing inflation and cost of living, and putting libraries in context. Each of these strategies is a proven success, and examples of their use are provided.

INTRODUCTION

Statistics. The mere word sends cold chills up backs, wipes smiles from faces, and silences a room faster than the mention of E. F. Hutton in their commercials. It recalls the purgatory of math classes and the sweaty-palmed dread of standardized tests. And, for all too many of us, it still makes our eyes glaze over as we ponder seemingly endless pages of numbers that are supposed to mean something to us, but do not. (Lance, 1991, p. 206)

This paper is about how library managers can use statistics in making decisions. It begins with a review of the many types of helpful data available to library managers. That is followed by a discussion of five strategies for using such statistics in library management. Each of these strategies is a proven success, so examples of their use are provided.

TYPES OF AVAILABLE DATA

Library managers can draw on five types of available data to inform their decision making: statistics on public and academic libraries and school library media centers, data on library salaries and benefits, employment outlook statistics for library workers, indexes of inflation over time and cost-of-living differences from place to place, and demographic and economic data on the people libraries serve.

Library Statistics

Although specific data elements collected from different types of libraries vary, there are some common categories of items in most collections: the population served (residents of a jurisdiction; students enrolled in a school, college, or university), staffing levels (usually distinguishing professionally trained or credentialed librarians from other staff), finances (income or expenditures), collection size by format, services provided (e.g., visits, circulation, reference, and interlibrary loan transactions), and, increasingly, output or performance measures (e.g., fill, reference completion, and document delivery rates).

These statistics are produced by individual libraries and compiled by state library and higher education agencies, the Library Statistics Unit of the National Center for Education Statistics (National Center for Education Statistics, 1992; Podolsky, 1991), professional library associations (e.g., Pritchard & Finer, 1991), individual researchers (e.g., Miller & Shontz, 1991) and the private sector (e.g., Quality Education Data, 1991).

In selecting a source of available data on libraries, seven questions should be answered:

Does this source cover the type and size of library on which data are needed? For example, the latest data on public libraries serving populations of 100,000 or more are available in the Public Library Association's (1991) *Public Library Data Service Statistical Report '91*, while data on larger university libraries may be found in the Association of Research Libraries *ARL Statistics* (Pritchard & Finer, 1991).

How current are the available data in question, particularly compared with how current they need to be for a given purpose? Of the two major annual reports of U.S. public library statistics, the Public Library Data Service (PLDS) statistical report is more current than the report generated by the Federal-State Cooperative System (FSCS) for Public Library Data, *Public Libraries in the 50 States and the District of Columbia* (National Center for Education Statistics, 1992).

How comprehensive and representative are the available data for the type and size of library in question? FSCS reports cover the entire universe of public libraries in the United States, while PLDS reports focus on those serving populations of 100,000 and over.

Are the available data collected from a defined universe of libraries? The FSCS project is developing a universe file of public library agencies. It will be the only source of such universe-defining data.

To what extent are the comparability and quality of data assessed by the data compiler? The FSCS project takes longer to produce a report than its PLDS counterpart because it requires that data be collected based on a strict set of definitions and compiled at the federal level only after it has passed numerous edit checks by the state library agencies.

Do available data provide the range of data needed? If one is looking for data on fill rates, community characteristics, or roles played by a public library, PLDS reports provide such data.

In what form and in what ways are the data available? PLDS reports provide print access to individual library data, but that project does not release its machine-readable data files. Instead, PLDS offers custom research services on a fee basis. FSCS reports include only summary data for the states and the nation, but machine-readable data files are available.

Library Salaries

Like statistics on library inputs and outputs, data on library salaries are available for most types of libraries, although such data on larger libraries of all types are more readily available.

The more familiar suppliers of these data for different library types are their own professional associations. The American Library Association (Lynch, Myers, & Guy, 1991) reports salaries for specific staff positions in larger public and most academic libraries; the Association of Research Libraries (Fretwell & Pritchard, 1991) reports salaries for staff of larger academic libraries; and the Special Libraries Association (1991) reports salaries for different types of staff in a wide variety of special libraries of all sizes. Results and analyses of these salary surveys appear in regular articles in appropriate journals (Brimsek, 1990; Lynch, 1991b).

Less familiar, but frequently more comprehensive sources of salary data are professional associations for the larger institutions of which libraries are part. The International City Management Association (1991) includes public library directors among the city officials for whom it collects salaries. These data are extracted from the *Municipal Year Book* each year and published in an article in *Public Libraries* (Lynch, 1991a). At least one of its state-level counterparts, the Colorado Municipal League (1991) also collects data on employee benefits, such as types of retirement plans, insurance, employer contributions, accrual rates for vacation and sick leave, and the like. The College and University Personnel Association (1991) collects salary data for library and other types of staff at academic institutions, and the National Education Association (1991) collects salary data for library media specialists as well as for other school workers.

In addition, many library surveys conducted by state library agencies collect salary data, usually for directors and starting librarians and, occasionally, for specific position titles (Boucher, Lance, & Crocker, 1991). The newest library salary survey is one for support staff. It began in 1989 and is reported the following year in the July/August issue of *Library Mosaics,* a journal specifically for library support staff (Martinez & Roney, 1990).

Some compilers of library salary data provide mean and median salaries for different positions in different sizes of libraries. Many also provide quartiles, percentiles, or averages for the highest and lowest 10 percent.

Employment Outlook Statistics

For five-year periods, the U.S. Bureau of Labor Statistics (1992) and state labor departments (Colorado Department of Labor and Employment, 1991) estimate current employment in hundreds of occupations and project numbers of new positions (growth), turnover in existing positions (separations), and total openings (growth plus separations). Both professional librarian and library assistant/ bookmobile driver are among these occupations. These figures are broken out in several ways, including geography (for the nation, by state, and, frequently if not always, for state planning districts or counties) and industry (e.g., public librarians are counted in public administration— i.e., government).

Indexes of Inflation and Living Costs

Analyses of budgetary trends from year to year for a given library are often thwarted by the eroding effects of inflation on the library's purchasing power. This is especially true where library materials are concerned. Book prices are inflated at a higher rate than general consumer prices, and periodical prices are inflated at an even higher rate than books. Library managers cannot afford to overlook these facts in making budget decisions. Comparisons of salaries from library to library are thwarted similarly because living costs can vary dramatically from place to place. So, library managers must also be prepared to adjust such figures for differences in living costs.

The index used most commonly to assess inflation is the consumer price index (U.S. Bureau of Labor Statistics, 1992). But this index is inadequate for most library purposes because it underestimates—sometimes grossly—the impact of inflation on materials budgets.

There are many different sources of average materials prices and price indexes. These include annual articles on books (Grannis, 1991b) and periodicals (Carpenter & Alexander, 1991), which provide the most current data, as well as reports of recent figures in the *Bowker Annual* (Bentley, 1991; Grannis, 1991a).

Managers of different types of libraries also have their own indexes to draw upon. Research Associates of Washington publishes the Higher Education Price Index and the Elementary-Secondary School Price Index (Research Associates of Washington, 1991; also Halstead, 1991). The former contains a subindex, the Library Price Index, which itself contains separate index scores for different portions of an academic library budget (e.g., staff, materials, equipment, contracted services). The latter contains subindexes for librarians (i.e., library media specialists) and materials by level (i.e., elementary or secondary) and format (e.g., books, periodicals, cassettes). There is no comparable index of prices for public libraries. However, the Library Research Center at the University of Illinois, Urbana-Champaign, produces the Index of American Public Library Expenditures annually (Palmer, 1991). This index is not nearly so pure a measure of inflation as the others, but it does break out comparable index scores for staff, materials, and other expenses.

Despite a common misconception, the consumer price index does not provide a basis for comparing living costs from place to place. For an index of cost of living, library managers must turn to the American Chamber of Commerce Researchers Association (American Chamber of Commerce Researchers Association [ACCRA], 1991), which publishes a quarterly cost-of-living index for all urban areas in the United States. (Sample uses of all of these indexes will be described later.) Notably,

ACCRA's monopoly in this area is about to be challenged by Research Associates of Washington (1992), which is publishing its own annual cost-of-living index report.

Demographic and Economic Data

As library funding grows tighter and tighter, it becomes increasingly important for libraries of all types to understand the different types of users they serve and how best to serve them. In such a climate, demographic and economic data on those a library serves can be invaluable. Yet, most library managers are unaware of the many available sources of such data on which they can draw at little or no cost.

The federal government is a major data producer. The U.S. Bureau of the Census, the U.S. Bureau of Labor Statistics, and the National Center for Education Statistics collect and make available staggering quantities of demographic and economic statistics on the general population.

To promote the use of U.S. Census data, every state has a State Data Center, which is responsible not only for facilitating use of U.S. Census data, but also for compiling and making accessible a variety of state and local data, and referring users to other state and federal agencies that make data available (U.S. Bureau of the Census, 1990). Besides simply providing data in print or machine-readable form, State Data Centers offer other services, including data mapping and locator services. Two examples illustrate these types of services.

The Minnesota State Planning Agency (1991), that state's State Data Center, has created an online data mapping system, DATANET PLUS, which can draw on most of the data available from the agency to produce professional presentation-quality maps in color at relatively modest cost. The DATANET PLUS mapping software is now available to every state library agency through the generosity of the National Commission on Libraries and Information Science and the National Center for Education Statistics.

Colorado's Site Selector and Electronic Atlas is a computerized locator service which, for example, permits a library manager to select any intersection at which a new branch library might be constructed and obtain any available data he or she desires for a one-, three-, or five-mile radius (Colorado Division of Local Government, 1990).

In addition to public sector data providers, there is a rapidly growing private sector data industry. Perhaps the leading company in this field, the Claritas Corporation, has assigned every zip code in the United States to one of 40 lifestyle clusters based on a phenomenal amount of data drawn from such diverse sources as the U.S. Census, voting records, lists of magazine subscribers, television ratings, and new product warranty surveys (Weiss, 1988). Through an exclusive contract with Claritas, Quality Education Data (1990) has had every public library and school library media center in the United States assigned to one of ten lifestyle types (collapsed from the original Claritas 40). Another exemplary firm, National Demographics and Lifestyles (1990), will analyze its data on an organization's clientele and profile them in terms of customized clusterings or market segments identified from that data.

STRATEGIES FOR USING STATISTICS IN MANAGEMENT DECISIONS

Library managers can utilize five strategies in using statistics to make management decisions: taking the user's point of view, comparing libraries, tracking trends and making projections, indexing inflation and cost of living, and putting libraries in context.

Taking the User's Point of View

In taking the user's point of view, library managers have three proven tactics from which to choose: the market basket approach, the competitive market, and the taxpayer's perspective.

Converting total statistics to per capita figures helps to make them somewhat more understandable but is really just a first step in adopting this strategy. The market basket approach involves "fleshing out" per capita figures by identifying specific examples of the types of use they enumerate. For example, instead of simply reporting that users borrowed an average of six circulating items per capita during a year, why not add the names of the six items that were borrowed most that year (Library Research Service, 1989)? Another way of making library statistics meaningful to the general public is to view them in the competitive market. For example, voters might be persuaded to support a sales tax increase for a library by suggesting how little its annual cost per household—about $17.00—would buy otherwise, such as one tankful of gasoline, one family meal at a fast food restaurant, one extra large pizza (Boulder Public Library, 1987). A third angle on presenting library statistics from the user's viewpoint is taking the taxpayer's perspective. For example, a library's annual budget might be put in perspective by considering how long users work to pay the taxes that support it. Tax Liberation Day usually falls in early May. One recent year, Colorado's public libraries celebrated Library Tax Liberation Day at 11:00 A.M. on January 1 (Library Research Service, 1988)!

Comparing Libraries

Comparing one library with another (or group of others) is probably the most popular strategy for using statistics to support management decisions. Important issues to consider when making comparisons include: how to identify "peers," whether to use data on individual libraries or groups of libraries, and, if using grouped data, whether to compare to the mean (average) or median (middle) value for the group.

For public libraries, peers are most often identified on the basis of population served, operating expenditures, or political structure (city, county, library district). For academic libraries and school library media centers, peers are usually selected on the basis of level (elementary versus secondary, community college versus university) or enrollment. Data on individual libraries may be ranked, mapped, and—if the group is not too large—charted. A recent *Wall Street Journal* article (Hirsch, 1991) used data from the Federal-State Cooperative System for Public Library Data to rank the 50 states and the District of Columbia on total public library operating expenditures per capita. These figures were also mapped.

Grouped data are often more useful rhetorically and usually lend themselves to being charted simply and dramatically. The American Library Association's annual *ALA Survey of Librarian Salaries* reports means and medians as well as first and third quartiles for public and academic libraries nationwide and in four regions—North Atlantic, Great Lakes and Plains, Southeast, West and Southwest (Lynch, Myers, & Guy, 1991). In addition, public library figures are reported for two population ranges (100,000 and over and 25,000-99,999), and academic library figures, by level (two-year college, four-year college, and university). Besides demonstrating the rhetorical value of grouped data, this widely quoted annual publication also illustrates the potential differences between means and medians. For example, in 1991, the mean salary for a beginning librarian in the North Atlantic region was $27,700; the median salary was only $24,000. When comparing such figures, one should be aware that means are sensitive to extreme cases, while medians reflect more typical figures.

Tracking Trends and Making Projections

Tracking trends is another popular strategy for using statistics in management decision making. One of its strengths is that it calls for local data only, avoiding the sometimes troublesome issues of locating comparable data on other libraries and identifying meaningful "peers." This strategy may be employed in a variety of ways: comparing a given statistic from an earlier year with the same statistic for a later year, comparing or contrasting change over time in one statistic with change in another statistic, and comparing or contrasting change over time in a single statistic for a given library with such change for another library or groups of libraries.

There are many excellent examples of this strategy. Here are two. For many years, the annual *Directory & Statistics of Oregon Public Libraries* (Scheppke, 1991) has included a series of charts reporting year-to-year trends on a variety of statewide statistics, including population served, circulation, reference questions, and interlibrary loans. An example of comparing libraries to each other and to change over time is provided by the Management Profiles produced by the Illinois State Library (ISL) for Illinois public libraries. The Library Research Center (LRC), as part of its Statistical Services Contract with the ISL compiles the annual public library statistics submitted by each individual library. In addition to other statistical reports and products, the LRC compiles selected statistics into a packet of information called a Management Profile (Library Research Center, 1991). The packet has three profiles, each designed to provide comparative information to Illinois public library directors. The first profile includes statistics about library operations; the second, financial statistics; and the third, a comparison of selected current statistics from the first two profiles to the average of each of two peer groups selected by population served and income and expenditures values. Each peer group includes ten libraries. The profiles track trends by comparing the same statistics from one year to another. Since the profiles are produced annually, library managers are also able to compare change in statistics for one library with change in the same statistics for a group of peer libraries. Three customized graphics are included with each packet illustrating the most significant comparisons.

Indexing Inflation over Time and Cost of Living from Place to Place

The price indexes described earlier are very useful when tracking fiscal trends. These indexes can (and should) be used to adjust dollar figures for inflation over time or cost-of-living differences from place to place. The customized statistical reports received by Illinois public libraries also include a line chart illustrating five-year trends for circulation and operating expenditures in actual and constant (1985) dollars (Library Research Center, 1991). A recent example of using a cost-of-living index to adjust for place to place differences is provided by the Library Research Service (1990). Starting librarian salaries for metropolitan public libraries in the western states were ranked and then re-ranked after adjusting them for cost-of-living differences using the index produced by the American Chamber of Commerce Researchers Association.

Although most price indexes report changes during the recent past, there are a few agencies that make projections about future price changes.

These figures can be very useful in projecting a library's future budget needs. A recent "Library Market Outlook" column in *Library Journal* (Selsky, 1991, p. 42) reported projected 1992 increases in consumer prices and book prices. When such index projections are unavailable, credible projections might be made by extrapolating from past changes, assuming there are no known conditions that would preclude doing so.

Putting Libraries in Context

A final strategy for using statistics in making library management decisions is putting libraries in context. In applying this strategy, there are three important steps: scanning the social, political, and economic environment, identifying issues of concern to critical decision makers (e.g., board members, voters), and finding and using creatively appropriate data.

In 1988, when Colorado's governor targeted state library programs to be cut in favor of support for a new Denver airport, economic development programs, and efforts to promote tourism, the Library Research Service (Lance, 1988) responded with the following statistics:

- As many Coloradans are registered to use public libraries as are registered to vote.
- Circulation of books and other materials by Colorado libraries outnumbers passenger traffic out of Stapleton airport two to one annually.
- Visits to Colorado libraries outnumber ski lift ticket sales six to one annually.
- Participants in cultural and educational programs sponsored by Colorado's public libraries each year would fill Mile High Stadium seven times and McNichols Arena 29 times.

FOR MORE INFORMATION

This paper has described a wide variety of available data on libraries and those they serve as well as several proven strategies for analyzing and presenting such data. The many bibliographies, directories, and how-to handouts that accompanied the presentation during the Allerton Institute may be obtained by writing to the following address: Library Research Service, 201 East Colfax Avenue, Room 309, Denver, Colorado 80203. Requests may also be made by telephone (303/866-6737) or fax (303/830-0793).

REFERENCES

American Chamber of Commerce Researchers Association. (1991). *Cost of living index. Second quarter* (Vol. 24, no. 2). Louisville, KY: ACCRA.

Bentley, S. (1991). Prices of U.S. and foreign published materials. In F. Simora (Comp. & Ed.), *Bowker annual library and book trade almanac 1991* (36th ed., pp. 399-422). New Providence, NJ: R. R. Bowker.

Boucher, J. J.; Lance, K. C.; & Crocker, M. K. (1991). *Statistics & input-output measures for Colorado public libraries, 1990.* Denver, CO: State Library and Adult Education Office.

Boulder Public Library. (1987). *The public bridge, 4*(5).

Brimsek, T. A. (1990). SLA biennial salary survey preliminary report. *Special Libraries, 81*(4), 338-340.

Carpenter, K. H., & Alexander, A. W. (1991). Price index for U.S. periodicals 1991. *Library Journal, 116*(7), 52-59.

College and University Personnel Association. (1991). *1990-91 Administrative compensation survey.* Washington, DC: CUPA.

Colorado Department of Labor and Employment. (1991). *Occupational employment outlook, 1991-1995.* Denver, CO: CDLE.

Colorado Division of Local Government. (1990). *Site selector & electronic atlas.* Denver, CO: DLG.

Colorado Municipal League. (1991). *CML benchmark employee compensation report.* Denver, CO: CML.

Fretwell, G., & Pritchard, S. M. (Comp. & Ed.). (1991). *ARL annual salary survey 1990.* Washington, DC: Association of Research Libraries.

Grannis, C. B. (1991a). Book title output and average prices: 1990 preliminary figures. In F. Simora (Comp. & Ed.), *Bowker annual library and book trade almanac 1991* (36th ed., pp. 423-433). New Providence, NJ: R. R. Bowker.

Grannis, C. B. (1991b). Title output in 1990 at record low. *Publishers Weekly, 238*(42), 31-34.

Halstead, K. (1991). Library price indexes for colleges and schools. In F. Simora (Comp. & Ed.), *Bowker annual library and book trade almanac 1991* (36th ed., pp. 388-399). New Providence, NJ: R. R. Bowker.

Hirsch, J. S. (1991, February 13). Many public libraries suffer major blows in local budget crisis. *The Wall Street Journal,* sec. A, p. 1, col. 1.

International City Management Association. (1991). *The municipal year book 1991.* Washington, DC: ICMA.

Lance, K. C. (1988). *The state library, regional library systems, and interlibrary cooperation: Investments in the information infrastructure of a more competitive and productive Colorado.* Denver, CO: Colorado State Library.

Lance, K. C. (1991). Building a sound case for support: Statistical evidence and its attractive presentation. In E. J. Josey & K. D. Shearer (Eds.), *Politics and the support of libraries* (pp. 206-217). New York: Neal-Schuman.

Library Research Center. (1991). 1989-90 Management profile, Mt. Vernon, C. E. Brehm memorial public library district. Urbana-Champaign, IL: University of Illinois.

Library Research Service. (1988, May 9). Tax liberation day! *Fastfacts: Recent statistics from the Library Research Service.* Denver, CO: State Library and Adult Education Office.

Library Research Service. (1989). A dollar's worth of value for every penny (bookmark). Denver, CO: State Library and Adult Education Office.

Library Research Service. (1990, November 21). High cost of living, low starting salaries for Colorado public librarians, 1990. *Fast facts: Recent statistics from the Library Research Service.* Denver, CO: State Library and Adult Education Office.

Lynch, M. J. (1991a). Salaries of library directors, July 1990: Data from the municipal year book 1991. *Public Libraries, 30*(4), 232-235.

Lynch, M. J. (1991b). Good news? Librarians' salaries increase an average of 7.6% for 1991. *American Libraries, 22*(10), 976.

Lynch, M. J.; Myers, M.; & Guy, J. (1991). *ALA survey of librarian salaries*. Chicago: American Library Association.

Martinez, E. B., & Roney, R. G. (1990). Library support staff salary survey 1990. *Library Mosaics, 2* (July/August), 8-12.

Miller, M. L., & Shontz, M. (1991). Expenditures for resources in school library media centers FY 1989-1990. *School Library Journal, 37*(8), 32-42.

Minnesota State Planning Agency. (1991). *DATANET PLUS user's manual*. St. Paul, MN: MSPA.

National Center for Education Statistics. (1992). *Public libraries in the 50 states and the District of Columbia, 1990*. Washington, DC: U.S. Government Printing Office.

National Demographics and Lifestyles. (1990). Brochure. Denver, CO: NDL.

National Education Association. (1991). *Estimates of school statistics 1990-91*. Washington, DC: NEA.

Palmer, C. (1991). Public library circ static, spending up 11.5%. *American Libraries, 22*(7), 659.

Podolsky, A. (1991). Academic library survey, 1988. In F. Simora (Ed. & Comp.), *Bowker annual library and book trade almanac 1991* (36th ed., pp. 448-505). New Providence, NJ: R. R. Bowker.

Pritchard, S. M., & Finer, E. (Comps.). (1991). *ARL statistics 1989-90*. Washington, DC: Association of Research Libraries.

Public Library Association. (1991). *Public library data service statistical report '91*. Chicago: Public Library Association.

Quality Education Data. (1990). Brochure. Denver, CO: QED.

Research Associates of Washington. (1991). *Inflation measures for schools & colleges*. Washington, DC: Research Associates.

Research Associates of Washington. (1992). *Wages, amenities, and cost of living: Theory and measurement of geographic differentials, 1990 data*. Washington, DC: Research Associates.

Scheppke, J. (1991). *Directory & statistics of Oregon public libraries*. Salem, OR: Oregon State Library.

Selsky, D. (1991). Book prices continue to rise faster than inflation. *Library Journal, 116*(2), 12.

Special Libraries Association. (1991). *SLA biennial salary survey 1991*. Washington, DC: SLA.

U.S. Bureau of the Census. (1990). *1990 census of population*, Vol. 1, *Characteristics of the population*, c. General social and economic characteristics. Washington, DC: U.S. Government Printing Office.

U.S. Bureau of Labor Statistics. (1992). The consumer price index—January (Monthly postcard). Washington, DC: U.S. Government Printing Office.

Weiss, M. J. (1988). *The clustering of America*. New York: Harper & Row.

NANCY A. VAN HOUSE

Acting Dean and Associate Professor
School of Library and Information Studies
University of California
Berkeley, California

Evaluation Strategies*

ABSTRACT

Evaluation is used for two major purposes: internal decision making
and communication with the external environment. An organization
may need very different approaches and strategies for these two. Much
of the work that has been done in library evaluation has been for internal
purposes. Evaluation is also important for an organization's relationship
with the environment that provides the resources the organization needs
to survive. A manager must convince the environment that the
organization's mission and goals are of value to the parent organization's
larger mission and that the organization is capable of achieving them.

INTRODUCTION

Bart Giamatti, discussing the state of higher education, says that
the greatest danger to the university is "the smugness that believes the
institution's value is so self-evident that it no longer needs explication,
its mission so manifest that it no longer requires definition and
articulation." Instead, he says, universities must be continually
challenged to justify themselves, to themselves and to the society that
they serve. They must be held accountable and urged to continually

*This paper has benefited substantially from my work with Thomas Childers and Charles
McClure on measurement and evaluation. Many of the ideas presented in this paper
are further developed in Childers and Van House (in press).

reexamine their presuppositions and their actions, lest "they stiffen up and lose their evolving complementarity to other American institutions" (Giamatti, 1988, p. 25).

One could easily substitute "library" every time Giamatti says "university." Evaluation is the process by which an organization examines, not only its actions, but its presuppositions, values, and mission. It is the process by which an organization holds itself accountable and by which it justifies its actions to its members and clients, to its funding agency, and to the larger public. Thoughtful evaluation can form the basis both for a careful self-examination of a library and for its conversation with its environment.

Evaluation is used for two major purposes: internal decision making and communication with the external environment. An organization may need very different approaches and strategies for these two (Childers & Van House, in press).

People make informal evaluations all the time, of all kinds of events, people, organizations, and objects. They compare their experiences with their expectations. Evaluation is made more formal and objective by making the process and the decisions more explicit and by collecting data on performance. A major rationale for formal, objective evaluation is to resolve, or at least to reduce, the differences in assessment that may result when more than one person is involved in an evaluation: agreement on the process, criteria, and evidence can reduce disagreement on conclusions.

THE EVALUATION PROCESS

The basic questions an organization must answer as a prerequisite to doing evaluation follow:

- What are the desired results of the program or activities being evaluated?
- How does the organization measure progress toward those ends?
- What produces the desired results?

This last question is the most difficult because it is a question of causality. How does an organization know what caused the results observed? How does management know whether, and which of, their actions created those results? How does the organization know what to do, or to do differently, in the future?

Figure 1 is the idealized evaluation process. It is idealized because an organization rarely performs all these steps in this order. Frequently, an organization begins evaluation only after a new program or service is implemented or when problems are suspected. But at that point it is assessing a moving target: the evaluation may miss the first effects of the project or program or lack evidence of how things were before problems developed.

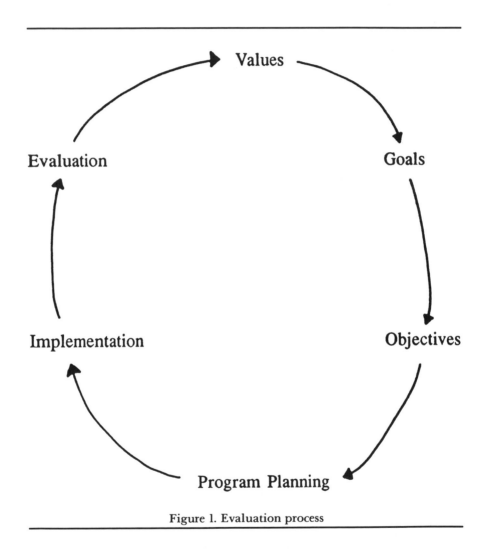

Figure 1. Evaluation process

The process portrayed in Figure 1 begins with values. These are determined by organizational or professional cultures. Wilson (1989), for example, notes that many organizations are composed primarily of people from one profession, which determines that organization's values and priorities. He uses the example of the Tennessee Valley

Authority, which was initially composed almost exclusively of engineers. They were interested in building dams and power plants, not environmental preservation.

Disagreement on values is most likely when more than one point of view is represented. Within an organization, disagreement is most likely when more than one profession is involved. Wilson gives the example of the U.S. Forest Service, in which the meaning of the "yield" of a forest is very different depending on who is talking: a biologist, a forester, an economist, or an engineer.

Based on their values (which may never be fully articulated, particularly if there is no disagreement within the organization) and on the politics of the situation (discussed below), decision makers establish an organization's mission and goals. Objectives make these concrete and measurable. How will the organization know whether it has met its goals? What is the evidence, the data, on which the evaluation will be based? Ideally, only once the mission, goals, and objectives have been identified does the organization determine the activities that it will undertake to achieve those goals.

Ideally, again, if the organization has not already collected data as part of a needs assessment, it collects baseline data before implementing a program: how can it know whether things have improved if it has not assessed where it is in the first place? Next, the organization evaluates the program or activities in question by collecting data to assess its progress on its goals and objectives.

Finally, the organization reconsiders its values, goals, objectives, and activities. Now that decision makers see what happened, are modifications needed? Are there unanticipated consequences? Unsuccessful activities?

An organization rarely follows this idealized process, however. An existing organization is a jumble of prior practice, ongoing programs, individual preferences and beliefs, and interest groups. What is useful about this idealized schema, however, is how it illustrates the underlying evaluation process.

In evaluation, disagreements are possible, even likely. A major use of the idealized, explicit evaluation process is that it often helps the participants to determine the roots of disagreement. Disagreement on an assessment, for example, may be a function of disagreement on values, unclear goals and objectives, differing assumptions about causality, or contradictory evidence on outcomes.

Several issues that are not addressed by this idealized description follow:

- How are values, goals, and objectives decided upon?
- Who are the decision makers, and whose preferences do they consider? What weight is given to different groups' preferences?
- Does an organization have a unified, identifiable set of goals and objectives? What about competing priorities? How are trade-offs made among them?
- How does the organization assess progress? What and how does it measure? What about goals that are not measurable?

These questions point out an important aspect of the evaluation process: evaluation is ultimately political. It depends on who is making the decisions and whose values and priorities are considered.

INTERNAL USES OF EVALUATION

The evaluation process of Figure 1 works best when the purpose of evaluation is to assess the success of activities in achieving identified goals and objectives. Evaluation is then used to inform resource allocation decisions. Should a program be instituted? Continued? Get more resources? Fewer? Is one course of action more successful than another? More cost-effective?

Other purposes (adapted from Weiss, 1972) include the following:

- Attention directing
- Problem solving
- Scorekeeping (How are we doing? Are we doing better or worse than before?)
- Conflict resolution (If two groups disagree on the value or effectiveness of activities or programs, an objective evaluation may resolve that disagreement.)
- Complacency reduction (An organization may overestimate its own effectiveness—objective evaluation may indicate problems.)
- Postponement or ducking responsibility (No action need be taken while an evaluation is being made.)
- Public relations
- Fulfilling grant requirements

These last two purposes lead into a discussion of the external uses of evaluation.

EXTERNAL USES OF EVALUATION

Evaluation is important for an organization's relationship with the environment that provides the resources the organization needs to survive

(Pfeffer & Salancik, 1978). An organization may use evaluation to communicate a variety of messages to its external environment for the following reasons:

- To justify its existence and its budget
- To explain what it does (What an organization measures determines to some degree what it can say about itself to others.)
- To demonstrate its priorities and concerns (The areas in which it sets objectives and monitors performance tell observers what its priorities are.)

Heymann (1987) says that a manager must convince his or her environment of two things: that the organization's mission and goals are of value and that the organization is capable of achieving them. This second point is worth emphasizing. Coming up with an acceptable mission is only the first step. The organization must also demonstrate its capacity to succeed.

Heymann (1987) goes on to say that those deciding whether to support an organization look at three things:

- What the organization does that affects their interests
- What its activities and interests say about what is important and whose interests are being considered
- What alliances the organization seems to be trying to build

Heymann's subject is the public sector, but his observations apply to any organization that needs the support of its environment. Special libraries in firms, for example, are generally not themselves profit centers, so they need the support of other parts of the organization in affirming the value of the library/information center to the parent organization's mission.

The related but separate processes of performing evaluation and reporting evaluation results are the means by which an organization communicates with and seeks to build support from its environment. For example, a police department that measures response time to calls demonstrates its concern for timely reaction. One that reports its educational contacts with the community demonstrates that its mission extends beyond crime detection and punishment to crime prevention and that it is building alliances with the public. A library that subdivides use figures by type of user (e.g., child versus adult) or type of service (branch versus main) implies that it is concerned with the types and distribution of services. A library that cannot report the time required to fill requests suggests that it does not care about timeliness of service.

The library's stakeholders include a wide range of groups with varying levels of interest in the library. Prominent among a library's stakeholders are the following:

- Users, who can be subdivided into numerous groups with differing needs and priorities
- Funders or the parent organization: the university, local government, the firm, whoever provides the library's support
- Staff, who are a critical resource and whose effort and energy are necessary for the library's success
- The public: members of the larger organization who are not necessarily library users (For academic libraries, this is faculty, students, and staff; for public libraries, this is the general public, especially taxpayers.)

What are stakeholders' concerns? Their concerns are of two types: library-specific concerns and more general concerns. For libraries that are public or quasi-public (e.g., libraries in private universities probably function more like publicly funded libraries than like corporate libraries), even people with no interest in the library per se examine the library through the lens of a set of ongoing concerns about the public sector (Heymann, 1987; Chase & Reveal, 1983). These include waste, corruption, and incompetence. The public and the press are always on the lookout for these failings in any public enterprise. In fact, people with no specific interest in the library are more likely to consider the library in this context because they may be more skeptical about the value of the library's services. The recent lengthy examination of university overhead charges, for example, has been front-page news because public money is at stake.

Public sector libraries also have to win the support of legislators at the appropriate levels of government. According to Heymann, legislators' major concerns are (a) the merits of the program or proposal, (b) what their stand would mean for their electoral support and influence on other matters, (c) the continued health of the legislative process itself, and (d) the demands of loyalty and friendship.

Similarly, appointed officials are concerned about the library's effect on their priorities: accomplishing their goals, being effective (and being seen as effective) in their jobs, and winning the support of the legislators. What this means is that the merits of the library itself are only one of several sets of concerns on which decisions are based.

More generally, libraries of all types are evaluated based on their contribution to their parent organization's larger mission and their effect on decision makers' other concerns, including power and influence relationships and the process by which decisions are made.

Every funder asks the larger question of why (and whether) the organization should support a library and at what level. What is the return on the investment in the library? Would those funds be better spent elsewhere? More than ever, the public sector—and the private sector as well—face endless, difficult trade-offs. Decision makers continually have to choose between allocating resources to the library or using them to meet other pressing needs.

For academic libraries, the question is what is the magnitude of their contribution toward the university's teaching and research (McClure, Van House, & Hert, 1991; Van House, 1990a; Koenig, 1990). For public libraries, the issue is their contribution toward solving community problems.

Tom Childers and I learned from the Public Library Effectiveness Study that public officials are concerned about the library's contribution to their larger community agendas (Van House, 1990b; Childers & Van House, in press). For example, one official was most interested in the library's literacy program. His priority was bringing jobs into the city, and employers need a literate work force. He did not care whether public libraries "should" be involved in literacy; his community had an urgent need that its library was addressing.

Decision makers are also concerned about how the library fits into ongoing patterns of power and influence. Typically, the library is just one of many areas in which they are making an ongoing series of decisions. The library is, in a sense, a temporary player in a continuing game by which resources are allocated and influence is exercised. A city council member in a city with district elections answered our questions about a controversial plan for a branch library by saying that he would defer to the council member in whose district the branch was located—as he would expect her to defer to him on decisions affecting his district (Van House, 1990b). The issue was not the library, but rather the power of council members over decisions affecting their districts.

External stakeholders also have concerns about library functions specifically. These concerns vary, but a major one is the collection. Does the library have the books and journals that people want? The prevailing public image of libraries of all types is as suppliers of materials. Librarians may see this as a naive and limited view, but that will not change the fact that this is most external observers' primary expectation of the library.

A critical issue in evaluation, particularly but not exclusively evaluation for communication with the external environment, is that the choice of the criteria by which an organization is to be evaluated is ultimately political. Each stakeholder group may have its own expectations and priorities. In fact, it is an oversimplification to assume that members of a group agree among themselves. The stakeholders may not themselves have consistent, rational, considered preferences, particularly if the library is not salient to their interests. And it is likely that different groups present the library with competing, equally valid preferences. The library has to decide which and whose preferences are to be considered, discover what those preferences are, and balance competing preferences and limited resources. All of which is likely to change rapidly, requiring a rapid, flexible response from the library.

INFORMATION FOR EVALUATION

Data are the objective evidence on which evaluation is based. Libraries typically measure the following:

- Resources
- Intensity of use of resources (e.g., circulation per volume)
- Internal processes (e.g., items cataloged)
- Output (e.g., circulation, reference transactions)
- Adequacy of performance relative to need (e.g., user success rates, circulation per capita)
- Availability
- Accessibility
- Cost to library
- Cost to client
- Outcomes

Moving down this list from inputs (resources) to outputs to outcomes, these concepts become more interesting and more difficult to measure. Traditionally, libraries have measured inputs and processes. More recently, they have begun to look more systematically at outputs (Van House, Lynch, McClure, Zweizig, & Rodger, 1987; Van House, Weil, & McClure, 1990).

What external evaluators are most interested in is outcomes, that is, the consequences of the library's actions, the effects of the library on the larger environment. Has the library made a difference in people's lives? For example, because of the library have the following occurred:

- Are students learning more?
- Are people finding jobs?
- Are workers more employable?
- Are people coping better with their life circumstances?
- Are researchers more productive?

The problem of demonstrating value is not unique to libraries, of course. In service organizations, in particular, where the outputs are intangible, the goals unclear, and effects often long delayed, it is difficult to measure results (Hasenfeld, 1983). Yet the commonly accepted model of rational resource allocation assumes that decision makers are searching for an optimal solution to the problem of maximizing goals (Feldman, 1989). Evaluation as libraries and other organizations have traditionally defined it is based on this model, which is of limited applicability.

OTHER INFORMATION FOR EVALUATION

If libraries cannot always measure the factors most of interest, particularly outcomes or impacts, and if they cannot define a unitary set of objectives to be maximized, what can be done?

First, research on library outcomes is needed. There is little, and most of it relates to special libraries or information in science and technology (Koenig, 1990). More needs to be done. This requires some serious thinking by librarians about what those impacts are, and how they can be identified and described to the library's external audience. This is not an easy task, but added efforts in this direction are essential.

Second, objective data are needed wherever possible. But the lack of objective measurement data in some areas does not mean that we have no information. In our interviews, Childers and I met city managers and city council members who had been youth-at-risk and attributed their success at least in part to the public library. They were now ardent supporters of the public library. Their own experiences had convinced them of the library's value, and they told persuasive stories.

Personal experience makes powerful stories. Anecdotal information can be used effectively with external decision makers (Childers & Van House, in press). It can also be used to guide research, to identify kinds of impacts to be assessed.

Third, even when information does not guide decision making, that does not mean that the information is not used. Often its greatest contribution is in interpretation, that is, in determining how people frame issues. Feldman (1989), in a trenchant discussion of the role of the policy analyst, points out that data gathering and analysis often precede or lag decision making. The model of rational decision making, by which decisions are based on data, is only one possible model, and it is often not applicable. However, what analysts often succeed in doing is affecting how people define and structure an issue and the alternatives that they consider—in short, the meaning that is assigned to the situation and the information.

The evaluation process and evaluative information can be useful in framing the discussion about what the library is and does and its contribution to the larger organization. Quantitative and qualitative information—measurement and anecdotes—can be used to guide the internal and external discussion and interpretation about the library, its outputs, and its contribution to the larger community.

REFERENCES

Chase, G., & Reveal, B. (1983). *How to manage in the public sector.* Reading, MA: Addison-Wesley.

Childers, T., & Van House, N. A. (in press). *What's good? Describing the public library's effectiveness.*

Feldman, M. S. (1989). *Order without design: Information production and policy making.* Stanford, CA: Stanford University Press.

Giamatti, A. B. (1988). *A free and ordered space: The real world of the university.* New York: W. W. Norton.

Hasenfeld, Y. (1983). *Human service organizations.* Englewood Cliffs, NJ: Prentice-Hall.

Heymann, P. B. (1987). *The politics of public management.* New Haven, CT: Yale University Press.

Koenig, M. E. D. (1990). Information services and downstream productivity. In M. E. Williams (Ed.), *Annual review of information science and technology* (Vol. 25, pp. 55-86). New York: Elsevier Science.

McClure, C. R.; Van House, N.; & Hert, C. (1991). *A new strategic direction for the AAHSLD annual statistics: Planning, service roles, performance measures, and management information systems for academic health science libraries: Final report for phase I.* (Prepared for Association of Academic Health Science Library Directors). Manlius, NY: Information Management Consulting Services.

Pfeffer, J., & Salancik, G. (1978). *The external control of organizations: A resource dependence perspective.* New York: Harper & Row.

Van House, N. A. (1990a). Library resources and research productivity in science and engineering: Report of a pilot study. In *Communications in support of science and engineering: A report to the National Science Foundation from the Council on Library Resources* (pp. IV B-1 - IV B-54). Washington, DC: Council on Library Resources.

Van House, N. A. (1990b). The public library effectiveness study: The unpublished story. *California Library Association Newsletter, 32*(12), 1, 13.

Van House, N. A.; Lynch, M. J.; McClure, C. R.; Zweizig, D. L.; & Rodger, E. J. (1987). *Output measures for public libraries: A manual of standardized procedures* (2nd ed.). Chicago: American Library Association.

Van House, N. A.; Weil, B. T.; & McClure, C. R. (1990). *Measuring academic library performance: A practical approach.* Chicago: American Library Association.

Weiss, C. H. (1972). *Evaluation research: Methods of assessing program effectiveness.* Englewood Cliffs, NJ: Printice-Hall.

Wilson, J. Q. (1989). *Bureaucracy: What government agencies do and why they do it.* New York: Basic Books.

JOE L. SPAETH

Professor
Department of Sociology and Survey Research Laboratory
University of Illinois at Urbana-Champaign

Perils and Pitfalls of Survey Research

ABSTRACT

The various stages of a survey—sampling, questionnaire design, and data collection—all present potential problems. Decisions about sampling include the type and size of the sample as well as the selection of the population to be sampled. In questionnaire design, there are a number of stages, including wording the questions, pretesting the questions, and finalizing the questions. After determining the questions to be asked, the advantages and disadvantages of different data collection types need to be considered—e.g., self-administered questionnaires, telephone interviews, or face-to-face interviews. A final concern is who will administer the survey.

INTRODUCTION

A survey is a very complex undertaking with ample opportunities for going wrong. Consider a brief list of some of the stages involved: research design, sampling, questionnaire design and construction, data collection, data processing, data analysis, and reporting. One of the problems is that the linear progress implied by the list is quite misleading. The design of the research must be influenced by the type of data analysis contemplated; if it is not, something is sure to go wrong at the end. The survey must ask the right questions in a way that is sensible to respondents; if not, there will not be the right data to analyze. A sample must at once be feasible to draw and reflective of the population that it is supposed to represent; if it is not, the information you produce could be irrelevant or, worse, misleading. Data collection presents a

63

whole set of problems of its own, one of which is getting an acceptable completion rate; if you do not, your sample is not what you think it is; you will not know *what* you are talking about because you will not know *who* you are talking about. In short, survey research is just one quality control problem after another. It is also a whole bunch of quality control problems at the same time.

SAMPLING

Sample Types

With sampling, there are a number of quality control problems and some solutions to those problems. There are two basic types of samples—samples of many and samples of one. Samples of many are the sort of thing people think about when they think about surveys. You want a lot of "representative" cases pertaining to the population you are interested in. Well-designed samples of many are known as probability samples because the probability that each element will fall into the sample is known.

Most people are also familiar with samples of one. When you write a paper, you may ask a colleague to criticize it. Writers know that they are poor judges of whether they have actually said what they meant to say. You do not choose your critic to represent any particular population—a sample of one could not do that anyway—you choose her or him to tell you about possible trouble spots. From that point of view, several samples of one are better than just one. Thus we have a third kind of sample, samples of several, which are basically accumulations of samples of one and which are used to look for and find trouble. Because surveys are so complex and involve so many different activities, using samples of several for quality control is particularly important.

Another kind of sample of several can masquerade as a sample of many. Known as convenience samples, their distinguishing characteristic is that there is no way to estimate the probability of an element's falling into the sample. A common example is freshmen in Psych 100 classes—unless you want a theory of freshmen in Psych 100 classes, in which case freshmen in Psych 100 classes at the University of Illinois would still be a convenience sample. There are lots of freshmen in Psych 100 classes, but if you are interested in saying something about a wider spectrum of humanity, that does not make any difference. No matter how many observations there are in a sample, if its observations are not drawn with known probability and if it does not correspond to the population you want to represent, you are still dealing with a convenience sample. The bottom line here is that a good small sample is better than a bad large sample.

Sample Size

A common question about sampling is: "How large should my sample be?" Unless there is one variable that you are interested in beyond all others, this is one of the hardest questions that you can ask a survey researcher. One answer is: "How much time or money do you have?" Another is: "It depends." It depends on how accurate you want your estimate to be. That is the easy part. It depends on what kinds of comparisons you want to make. If you want to compare men and women, you can let the chips fall where they may because each is roughly half of the population. If you want to compare blacks and whites, you need to begin thinking about drawing a supplemental sample of blacks because the usual sample has about nine times as many whites as blacks. Unfortunately, your comparisons will basically be as valid as your sample of blacks. It therefore makes sense to allocate some of your resources to increasing the number of blacks at the expense of decreasing the number of whites. Since finding blacks is costlier than finding whites, you might not aim for a 50-50 distribution. There are actually formulas that will tell you what the optimal distribution is, as long as you can estimate how much it will cost to collect data from each subgroup. (An excellent reference for problems of this kind is Leslie Kish [1987], *Statistical Design for Research.*)

Population Selection

Now for some of the perils and pitfalls—and also some of the opportunities—in sampling. As you know, samples are necessary because it is usually too expensive and time consuming to enumerate an entire population. The U.S. Census does a Post-Enumeration (sample) Survey (PES) in order to evaluate the completeness and accuracy of the enumeration. As you will remember, the Secretary of Commerce made news last summer by deciding to stick with the enumeration, even though the PES showed that the Census had an undercount of about 5 million people. The professionals at the Census Bureau would have gone with the PES.

One of the research design problems that you must solve is exactly what population you want to represent. This is usually not a simple issue. Take trying to draw a sample of the users of a library. For public libraries, there are cardholders, and presumably the modern, computerized library has a list of cardholders from which a sample could be drawn. But what about people who use the library but do not have a card? At least two such groups spring immediately to mind. There are the people who come in on Saturday morning to read their hometown newspapers, but never check out a book. The twin cities— Champaign and Urbana, that is—have a public library each. I have a Champaign library card but have checked out books from Urbana. That makes me a user of the Urbana Free Library. If Urbana wanted to survey their users, should they care about people like me or people from farther afield who have access to the Urbana library?

The reason I raise questions like this is not that there is a single, right answer; there is not. However, you must decide in advance what population you want to represent and why. Then, of course, you must also decide whether there is a list or a way of creating a list of the population that you really want to sample, so that you can draw your sample elements from the list. Often there is not, and then you must decide how seriously your purposes are diluted by the compromises you have to make in order to get some kind of sample to collect data from.

Unless you are the U.S. Census doing the decennial enumeration or a survey evaluating that enumeration, you are not likely to draw a sample of the United States that represents the *entire* population. Guam is very likely to be left out; Alaska and Hawaii often do not make it either. Probably more important, even large-scale government surveys like the Current Population Survey, which estimates the unemployment rate for states and localities, refer to the "civilian, noninstitutionalized" population. If you were in the armed forces living on base, in jail, or living in a college dormitory, your chance of falling in such a sample would be zero.

I mention this point partly to indicate that everybody makes compromises but mostly to point out that there comes a time when it becomes useful to think about combining different survey designs and therefore different surveys to represent a particular population. If you really wanted to include everybody—and could afford to do so— the solution for the U.S. population would entail doing several basically independent surveys, one for the civilian noninstitutionalized population, one for service personnel, one for college students, another for prisoners, and still others for other institutionalized groups.

I should also mention the problems with publicly available lists. They are often pretty bad because they are incomplete and out of date. Because there are few unlisted telephones in this area, the Champaign-Urbana white pages include over 90 percent of the households in the twin cities. The small percentage without phones would have been omitted, as would anybody who had moved in after the listing was compiled. Thus, the Champaign-Urbana directory would be adequate for many purposes; however, it would be a bad sampling frame if you were interested in providing outreach to newcomers. If you were interested in doing a survey of Chicagoans, the white pages would be abysmal for just about any purpose. The nonlisting rate in Chicago is something like 40 percent.

There are many other kinds of directories. Some are better than others, and sometimes there are ways of telling how good a directory is. For example, there is a published list of drugstores; it contains about 50,000 entries. The census has enumerated drugstores, as well as other business enterprises, and estimates that there are about 50,000 drugstores in the United States. The list would therefore be adequate for most purposes. The American Library Association (ALA) has a directory of members. It turns out, however, that not all librarians—not even all professional librarians—are members of the ALA, at least according to the census. What we have here is a separate research problem. Which kinds of librarians tend to be members of the ALA and which do not? If you do not know, a sample of librarians based on the ALA directory could be quite misleading.

You may be wondering whether large-scale samples of several could ever be useful—I hesitate to say valid. We have already seen that for finding trouble spots in questionnaires, samples of several are useful. If you are looking for trouble, samples of several can be useful on a larger scale. A couple of years ago, a survey on date rape was done on the Urbana campus, with a response rate of about 37 percent. It revealed that date rape was quite a frequent event and therefore a serious problem. With two possible respondents missing for every one who provided data, it would have been a mistake to attempt a numerical estimate of the incidence of date rape. On the other hand, the rate was so high that, even in the unlikely event that all the nonrespondents had not experienced date rape, it would indicate the existence of a serious problem.

There are other uses for samples of several. Let me outline a sneaky one that should be of particular use to academic librarians. Journals are not only getting more expensive, they are proliferating. It would seem to make sense to eliminate some little used journals so that the more widely used ones can continue to be supported. How to do this? Send out a self-administered survey to faculty members and ask them what journals are crucial to their research. You will have a fairly low response rate, and lots of journals will not be mentioned at all. When the inevitable complaints are made, say, "You had your chance to tell us what you wanted, and you didn't take it." Duck.

That is the bad news (only part of it, actually). There *is* good news. A surprising number and range of sampling problems have legitimate solutions. If you wanted, you could sample the fish in a pond and come up with an estimate of the number of fish in that pond. You could sample clouds so that you could seed some and not others. You could estimate the number of homeless in a community. You could also sample a variety of other rare or hard to reach populations, such as people who had a particular form of cancer, veterans of Operation Desert Storm, or work organizations of all types and sizes.

The University of Illinois is fortunate to have one of the world's foremost experts in the sampling of human populations, Seymour Sudman. His book, *Applied Sampling*, is an excellent and accessible introduction to the topic, and a recent article that he coauthored in *Science* outlines a variety of ways to sample rare or hard to reach populations (Sudman, 1976; Sudman, Sirken, & Cowan, 1988). In short, if you have a sampling problem, consult a sampling expert. There are lots of ingenious ways of producing a probability sample, even when a convenience sample may seem the only way to go.

QUESTIONNAIRES

Asking Questions

Even when you have an adequate list or a good substitute for one, your problems are far from solved. You must draw your sample and then obtain data from as many of the elements in it as possible, and you must get your respondents to answer the right questions. I will discuss the problems of data collection later. First I want to examine some of the problems and pitfalls in asking questions and getting valid answers to them.

For the most part, I am talking about factual questions—questions to which there is a real answer that you could learn if you only had access to the right data, like official records. Of course, there are lots of problems with attitudinal questions; I am simply assuming here that you are most likely to want the facts. Factual questions have lots of problems of their own.

Let's start with the classical problems, the ones covered in most textbooks. You all know that you should not ask loaded questions or double-barreled questions, and that you should keep your questions simple. It is easy to find examples of bad questions that violate these principles, and some of them are kind of fun—like this one purportedly asked of French coal miners by Karl Marx: "Does your employer or his representative resort to trickery in order to defraud you of a part of your earnings?" (Babbie, 1990, p. 43). The loading is pretty obvious— "trickery," "defraud," and also "resort." The question is also double-barreled. Why just trickery? What about brute force? Or, for something completely different, employees of the University of Illinois will recognize that trying to get money out of the legislature is a good way to keep salaries down. "Do you favor keeping the library open past midnight?" is also a loaded question. A better wording would be: "Do you favor or oppose keeping the library open past midnight?"

I want to call your attention to another bad question in order to make a point not made so frequently in the textbooks. This one was asked by a British Royal Commission just after World War II: "Has it happened to you that over a long period of time, when you neither practised abstinence, nor used birth control, you did not conceive?" (Moser and Kalton, 1972, p. 321). There is a whole catalog of things wrong with this question. It is too long; it is too complex; it uses big, Latinate words when smaller or at least English words would do— "practised abstinence," "conceive." It includes three negatives. The underlying mistake was this: the researchers were trying to get respondents to operationalize their (the researchers') research question in their (the researchers') words. Ordinary people cannot do this, and no one should expect them to. The example I have just given is an obvious one. Sometimes the problem is not so obvious, but you should be aware of it.

Those were some of the classical problems with factual questions. There are many more. Take social desirability. It turns out that having a library card is a socially desirable behavior. That is, if you ask members of a community whether they have a library card, more people will say that they have one than actually do. Then there are socially undesirable behaviors, like drinking. People tend to underestimate— or at least underreport—the amount of drinking that they do.

There has also been a fair amount of research on the memory problems involved in answering survey questions. One of these problems is telescoping. Let me illustrate from personal experience. The question is: "Did you visit the library in the past month?" Leaving aside the possibility that I should have been asked about the Champaign library, the Urbana library, and the University library, preferably separately, what is my answer? These words were written on July 27, and I will stick to that date because it is a useful reference point. In late June, I was involved in interviewing respondents to a survey of mine that was in the field at the time and in preparing to go on vacation. Somewhere around the end of June, I went to the Champaign library to get some books on the area we were going to visit and to the University library to look up the address of a potential respondent. Several things are involved here. When was the last time I went to a library? Was it before or after June 27? I cannot remember. What would I have said if I had actually been asked? I could easily have said "Yes" on the grounds that I knew I was using the library at about the right time. If I had not used the library after June 27, I would have been telescoping.

I would have reported doing something during one time period when I had actually done it during an earlier one. This is a common problem when respondents are asked to recall the timing of things that they have done or that have happened to them.

Another problem is that some things are not important enough—to the person—for them to remember. Until I started thinking about it, I had forgotten about my visit to the University library. Even though I have told other people about it in other contexts, the visit itself was so brief (albeit successful) that I might easily have forgotten it in the context of being asked in a survey interview.

One lesson here is that if you are interested, say, in the ways that people can use a library, you need to come up with a list of those ways and ask your respondents about each specifically. This will give you better data than a single, general question. You will still probably underestimate most types of usage, but not as badly. The last item on your list will be something like: "Anything else?" Given the list, your estimate of the usages not on the list will be even worse than if you had just asked one general question.

I have used such a detailed list in a survey that investigated the extent of volunteer activities in Champaign County. The questionnaire began with a list of 17 different types of organizations for which people could volunteer. Using this list, we estimated that about 75 percent of the adult residents of Champaign County had volunteered to do something for somebody. A survey done elsewhere had asked one general question on volunteering, and this question produced an estimate of about 50 percent. There is good reason to believe our estimate. When we asked a general question about monetary contributions, we came up with about the same estimate as the other study did.

Questionnaire Design

The idea of samples of one or several is very important here. Designing a questionnaire is one activity in which more heads are definitely better than one. The first phase of questionnaire design is figuring out what research questions you want answered. The second is trying to formulate specific questionnaire items that will help you answer the research questions. After you have come up with a tentative questionnaire draft, you need to show it to other people, including if possible survey professionals, who have a lot of experience with asking questions. No one person can think of all the ways in which it is possible for a respondent—or for different kinds of respondents—to misinterpret a question. At this stage, you need all the help you can get—and it still probably will not be enough.

A further stage, if you have the resources, is to try your questions out on a small number of people and ask them to help you look for trouble. This is where focus groups come in. You can get focus group members to tell you what a question means to them or which questions cause them trouble. You can also ask people to think aloud when they are answering a question. That is basically what I was doing when I was talking about the timing of my library visits this summer.

Next, you must pretest your questionnaire—in other words, try it out on real people. In contrast to focus groups, the pretest is a kind of dress rehearsal. It is standard practice, therefore, not to tell respondents that you are doing a pretest. Nevertheless, the goals of a pretest are different from those of the main survey. The purpose of a pretest is still to look for trouble—for problems. You should not have any difficulty finding them. One of the good things about real people is that they have virtually an infinite capacity for surprising you. The sample-of-several principle is clearly important here. Pretests are usually small and often not based on probability sampling. You want to give people the opportunity to interpret each question as they see it. If a respondent interprets a question in a way that never occurred to you, you need to fix the question. At the same time, it is important to get all the bugs you can out of a questionnaire before you pretest it. If the pretest reveals a lot of problems that require fixing, you will need to do another pretest. After all, you have just changed your questions, and the new ones could have new problems. (Good treatments on questionnaire design and question wording include Stanley Payne [1951], *The Art of Asking Questions*, a classic in the field; Howard Schuman and Stanley Presser [1981], *Questions and Answers in Attitude Surveys*; and Seymour Sudman and Norman Bradburn [1982], *Asking Questions*.)

Even after taking all the precautions you can, your questionnaire will still be open to misinterpretation, but there comes a stage after which preliminary research has diminishing returns. That means that the surprises are still out there waiting to happen. One such surprise happened in one of my research projects and has achieved a certain notoriety in the trade. In 1961 I was in charge of a project that investigated attitudes toward the Eichmann trial among residents of the San Francisco Bay Area. There were several questions designed to measure respondents' awareness and knowledge of the trial, including the first ones, which asked respondents whether they were aware of ten events that were in the news at the time. The third event was the Eichmann trial. One day an interviewer came back to the office to explain why he had gotten a refusal. When he knocked on the door, a woman answered and he began the interview. Question 3: "Have you heard or read of the Eichmann trial?" The lady replied: "I think President Eichmann is doing a fine job" and slammed the door. You win some and you lose some. If you do not use samples of several to help you design your questionnaire, you will lose a lot more than you need to.

Since I have had to leave out more than I could possibly put in, you will notice that I have not said much about the research design phase as such and that I therefore have not said anything about that basic activity, the review of the literature. In the usual sense, I am still not going to say anything about it. I do recommend, however, that you look for other people's questionnaires and questions, if any exist on your topic. For one thing, if you use their questions, you will have the opportunity to compare your situation with theirs. For another, their questions have presumably undergone some of the tests to which you will submit yours. To some extent, therefore, they are "pre-pretested." Nevertheless, you will still need to pretest these questions in the context of *your* questionnaire. Still, as far as questions are concerned, heed the immortal word of Tom Lehrer: "Plagiarize." (Given the attention that plagiarism has received in the media lately, this may seem like dubious advice, but in designing questionnaires plagiarism is legitimate.)

DATA COLLECTION

When it comes to data collection, a whole new set of perils and pitfalls opens up. As you know, the three basic types of data collection are self-administered questionnaires, telephone interviews, and face-to-face interviews. They share some problems, but each has its own problems as well. One of these shared problems is actually achieving the sample that you designed and drew. Another is making certain that each question is answered—adequately and accurately.

Response Rate

The measure of how well you have achieved the sample that you drew is known as the response rate. It is simply the number of completed questionnaires divided by the total number of eligible possible respondents who fell in your sample. It is usually expressed as a percentage. In telephone and face-to-face interviewing, response rates of 70 to 80 percent are common. Response rates to self-administered surveys range much more widely than this, although it is possible to achieve a response rate of 70 percent or even higher.

Let's think about response rates for a minute. If your response rate was 90 percent (and federal surveys commonly have response rates at least that high), you would have nine times as many respondents as nonrespondents. Missing 10 percent of the cases that you wanted would not be a serious handicap. The missing people would have to be very different from the ones that you collected data on for their absence to have much effect on your estimates of population parameters. A response rate of 75 percent is not as good, but you still would have three times as many respondents as nonrespondents. You can see why a response rate of 50 percent is horrible. Now you have as many nonrespondents as respondents. If the two groups differ on the variables you are interested in, your results could be quite distorted. Many self-administered questionnaires have response rates in the 20s and 30s. If, heaven forfend, that is what you get, you have wasted your time and money. There are ways of increasing response rates to self-administered surveys, and I will go into some of them in a little while.

First, I should warn you against a couple of common practices, one being a form of cheating and the other a kind of pious hope that looks good but does not perform too well. The first is using replacement respondents. Say you want a sample of 500, but your best efforts have yielded only 400. Why not draw a new sample and pick up the extra 100 cases? Your first 400 were cooperative, and the missing 100 were not. Your new sample of 100 will also be cooperative. If cooperation is related to the variables you are interested in, you have a biased sample. You are not adding 100 cases worth of new information.

The cheating comes in if you were to take your second 100 cases from a large pool. What would your response rate be? Say you actually drew another 500 possible cases, and you needed to try something like 150 to get your 100 interviews. You certainly would not count the 350 people you never approached in the denominator of the response rate, would you? When supplementary sampling of this kind is done, response rates often go unreported. If a response rate is reported, it is likely to be misleading.

The second practice is known as weighting. Say you have achieved a response rate of 50 percent but that you know from other sources the distribution of your population on certain key variables, like age, sex, place of residence, and education. You discover that the distribution of your sample on these variables differs from the distribution in the population. Your sample is likely to be older, more female, more rural, and better educated than the population. You might think that you could correct for these biases by weighting your sample so that its distribution corresponds to the population distributions. This procedure helps, but research has shown that it by no means completely corrects for whatever biases may exist.

Self-Administered Questionnaires

Since most users of libraries are literate and since self-administration *seems* to be the least expensive method, I will devote most of my remaining remarks to that method. As I said, response to self-administered questionnaires varies all over the lot. A major factor influencing the cost of gaining cooperation and the degree of nonresponse is whether the questionnaire can be administered to groups or must be administered to individuals. If all or practically all members of a group are present, the response rate is likely to be high, and the larger the group, the lower the per-questionnaire cost of collecting data. If, on the other hand, there are many absences, alternative methods must be tried, and the cost advantages diminish considerably. A problem with group administration is that some people are likely to fall into your sample more than once. If your groups were classes at the University of Illinois and you drew a sample of classes, some students would be in more than one of the classes that you sampled. You would need some way of identifying respondents and culling out the duplicates so that no one would be represented more than once.

You might expect that a self-administered questionnaire distributed and filled out by mail might be very cost-effective, but the problems of collecting data by mail make some, but not all, of the cost-effectiveness illusory. It would be very unusual for you to send out a questionnaire and get a 75 percent response rate to the first mailing. The 1990 census got about a 60 percent response to its first mailing. Except in comparison with earlier censuses, this is quite a remarkable degree of cooperation. You and I would be doing well to get a 40 percent response rate. Therefore, in your planning, you must include time and money to do follow-up mailings. If, after two or three weeks, you have not received a questionnaire from someone in your sample, you should send out another questionnaire. If, after another two or three weeks, you have not received a questionnaire, send out another one.

My own rule of thumb is that a follow-up mailing will produce about half as many completed questionnaires as its immediate predecessor. Thus, given an initial 40 percent response rate, you could expect to get about 20 percent more from the first follow-up and 10 percent more again from the second, for a total of 70 percent, which verges on the respectable. Note, however, that a 30 percent initial response would ultimately yield only 52.5 percent, which verges on the awful. Then what?

Sending out questionnaires to nearly half of your sample (a third follow-up) in order to get a 3 percent response is clearly not worth it. (Remember the sequence—30, 15, 7 and a half, 3 and a quarter.) If you are using the mails, you have names and addresses for the people in your sample. If you have phone numbers, you can call people up and try to interview them. Now we are beginning to talk about real money. There is at least a partial solution to the money problem—sampling. If you were to draw a 10 percent sample of your nonrespondents and interview them by telephone, you would have a gross response rate of about 57 percent, still not very good. However, you could weight the responses of your telephone respondents by a factor of 10 and come up with something that more closely approximated a decent sample. You will remember that I was not enthusiastic about trying to match a sample to its population on the basis of known distributions of variables in the population. Here we have a somewhat different case. It rests on the following general principle: a probability sample of a probability sample is a probability sample.

You will have noticed that the procedures I have been recommending require that you be able to identify all respondents. This potentially raises a whole host of ethical issues. If each questionnaire has a unique serial number on it, as it should, respondents will know that you are keeping track of them. Clearly, respondents will not be anonymous. How important is this? There is some controversy on this subject, and it may be the case that on some issues guaranteeing anonymity is important. In general, however, I think that such a guarantee is neither necessary nor desirable. You should level with respondents. Tell them that you need to keep track of them in order to do a follow-up mailing, if necessary. This could encourage some people to respond, including a statistician named Harry Roberts, and me.

Roberts has named and promulgated the Roberts Rule for responding to self-administered questionnaires. If you get a questionnaire in the mail, throw it out. If you get a follow-up questionnaire, fill it out. That is also what I do. I do not know whether Roberts would violate his own rule if he believed that he would get a follow-up questionnaire; I probably would.

Face-to-Face Interviewing

I should also mention some of the problems connected with face-to-face and telephone interviewing. You may be surprised to hear that, except in rare circumstances in which you want to collect information in depth from a relatively small sample, I recommend against face-to-face interviewing. Anything on a large scale is likely to be extremely expensive. A statewide or nationwide study would virtually require using a professional survey organization. On that scale, developing and implementing a sampling design alone would blow most budgets out of the water. Furthermore, face-to-face data collection is extremely inefficient. Only about half the time an interviewer spends in the field is spent doing interviews. The rest is spent in travel. Just getting to where the interview is supposed to take place can take a lot of time.

Furthermore, it is often necessary to return to a household in order to interview a specific respondent. If so, even more time is spent getting there and getting back.

There has been considerable research on the differences between collecting data face-to-face and by telephone, with inconclusive results. In other words, conventional wisdom to the contrary notwithstanding, there are few if any advantages to face-to-face interviewing. One clear one is that in telephone interviewing, respondents cannot be presented with visual stimuli, and interviewers cannot observe characteristics of the housing unit or neighborhood.

Telephone Interviewing

Telephone interviewing has advantages of its own. First, it is cheaper. Interviewer time can be used much more efficiently. If someone is not home, it is easy to try a different number. If the right respondent is not there, a callback can be arranged in a few minutes. Furthermore, in a well-run telephone setup, all of the interviewers will be in the same place, and they can be given standardized training and subject to constant, consistent supervision. There are therefore some real advantages to telephone interviewing.

One set of points is worth stressing. If you are going to use interviewers, they must be selected, hired, trained, and supervised. They must be taught general principles of interviewing, and they must be instructed in the goals and procedures of any given study. In telephone interviewing, a supervisor should monitor at random the work of every interviewer. In face-to-face interviewing, this is not possible. In both methods of data collection, the interview itself should be edited, first by the interviewer and then by a supervisor. Unsuccessful interviewers should be trained or let go. Note the last point. If you have hired and are paying interviewers, you can fire them. This is an important step in quality control. If you are using volunteers, or staff members whose real job is something else, you may not be able to get rid of them. The volunteers who quit are not necessarily going to be the bad interviewers, and the ones who stay are not necessarily going to be the good ones. (A good reference on data collection is Donald Dillman [1978], *Mail and Telephone Surveys: The Total Design Method.*)

CONCLUSION

Enough of my catalog of woes; let me summarize. Before doing a survey, you need to go through a series of steps, like the following: What is the question—what do I want to know? What is the answer—

how will I know when I have found out? Will a survey help? Who should be surveyed? Can I ask them questions that they can answer and that will help me to answer my questions? Is there a list or some other device from which I can draw a sample of all the whatevers that may be out there in the real world? If there is a list, how good is it? How serious is the fact that it is not very good? How can I get the people in the sample to cooperate with my survey? Who is going to process and analyze the data? Do I have the resources to do a decent survey? Do I have the time to do it myself? What kind of staff do I have that might be able to help me? Will we discover that the survey is consuming us?

Hiring somebody else to do the survey is likely to be costly. On the other hand, it is likely to take less time than if you did it yourself. The product is likely to be substantially better, and you will not discover for yourself how frustrating it is to do a survey with inadequate resources.

Whether you can afford to hire a survey organization to do the entire survey or not, the bottom line is: Get Help. Coming from a Survey Research Lab as well as a Sociology Department, I firmly believe in a codicil to the bottom line: Get Professional Help.

REFERENCES

Babbie, E. R. (1990). *Survey research methods* (2nd ed.). Belmont, CA: Wadsworth.

Dillman, D. A. (1978). *Mail and telephone surveys: The total design method.* New York: Wiley.

Kish, L. (1987). *Statistical design for research.* New York: Wiley.

Moser, C. A., & Kalton, G. (1972). *Survey methods in social investigation* (2nd ed.). New York: Basic Books.

Payne, S. L. (1951). *The art of asking questions.* Princeton, NJ: Princeton University Press.

Schuman, H., & Presser, S. (1981). *Questions and answers in attitude surveys: Experiments on question form, wording, and context.* New York: Academic Press.

Sudman, S. (1976). *Applied sampling.* New York: Academic Press.

Sudman, S., & Bradburn, N. M. (1982). *Asking questions: A practical guide to questionnaire design.* San Francisco, CA: Jossey-Bass.

Sudman, S.; Sirken, M.; & Cowan, C. D. (1988). Sampling rare and elusive populations. *Science, 240*(4855), 991-996.

JANE B. ROBBINS

Professor and Director
School of Library and Information Studies
University of Wisconsin-Madison

Affecting Librarianship in Action: The Dissemination and Communication of Research Findings

ABSTRACT

Issues and problems related to and techniques for improving communication between practitioners and researchers in librarianship are presented. The underlying assumption of this essay is that research, when designed with the practitioner in mind and communicated specifically to the practitioner, will positively affect the practice of librarianship.

INTRODUCTION

Communication of research is simply the systematic presentation of the systematic investigation of a problem. The research process is *not* complete until it has been reported. How it is reported depends upon the purpose of the research; it may be appropriate to communicate results in a variety of ways. For example, reports at meetings, technical reports, books, or journal articles either for the researcher or the practitioner community may be the most appropriate form.

The most important aspect of communicating research is that it be through a reaccessible package—presently primarily the journal article or book—indexed or abstracted by one of the services organized for those purposes. The reasons research must be accessible follow:

1. so others can determine the validity and reliability of the process used;
2. so others can replicate the research or create new projects from that research;
3. so that a contribution to knowledge is made; and
4. so that the number of those who know is increased, thereby increasing the likelihood that knowledge will be further increased.

Most researchers communicate their research because they have been educated to know that the research process is not complete until publication takes place. Most researchers also publish (a) because there is something new to say or because there is a new way of saying it, (b) for prestige, (c) for survival, (d) because someone asked that it be done, or (e) because the researcher simply cannot help him or herself.

Asking why researchers transmit their findings is somewhat similar to asking why the consumer of research consumes it. There can be many reasons, including (a) simply to increase their knowledge store, (b) in hopes that it may be useful knowledge in the future, or (c) in hopes that it will be useful in solving a problem immediately at hand.

PROBLEMS IN THE DISSEMINATION OF RESEARCH RESULTS

Historically, the mainstream of librarianship has not been oriented toward the systematic search for knowledge regarding information production, storage, dissemination, and use. Many practitioners view neither theory nor research as necessary bases for reliable and valid knowledge. The knowledge base is rather developed from previous practice, authoritative pronouncement, and intuition; however, there is now a growing research sophistication in the profession. This growing sophistication has been brought about by a number of factors: the importance of information to today's society; shrinking research resources forcing researchers to find new ways to select, acquire, disseminate, and use information; institutional demands for accountability in resource use; a larger number of doctoral level educated information professionals (although there needs to be an increasing number of doctoral educated individuals to replace the many reaching retirement age); and a growing number of individuals in related disciplines becoming interested in addressing information problems.

RESEARCHERS AND PRACTITIONERS: TWO WORLDS

Most fields have become seriously bifurcated into researcher versus practitioner communities. Both communities must strive to unfreeze this situation of "two cultures." As conceptualized by Donald Schön, professional knowledge is generally thought to best be understood from a hierarchical model: basic science, applied science, followed by skills and attitudes of practitioners as they perform their services. Research is considered to be "institutionally separate from practice, connected to it by carefully defined relationships of exchange. Researchers are supposed to provide the basic and applied science from which to derive techniques for diagnosing and solving the problems of practice. Practitioners are supposed to furnish researchers with problems for study and with tests of the utility of research results. The researcher's role is distinct from . . . the role of the practitioner" (Schön, 1983, p. 26).

Most practitioners and researchers will agree that the purpose of information research is to contribute to the body of knowledge that will ultimately allow, for want of a better phrase, "things to get better." Most practitioners and researchers generally agree that "good" research is able to fulfill that purpose; however, many factors militate against the development of sufficient knowledge about and understanding of research to allow meaningful communication between the two groups to take place. Some of the key militating factors follow:

1. Researchers too often identify problems worthy of being solved by talking only with other researchers, ignoring or overlooking the importance of identifying problems to be solved with practitioners.
2. Practitioners too often cannot identify researchable problems when requested to do so.
3. Researchers too often use language when communicating with practitioners that is not required and is not understandable to practitioners, not because practitioners are lacking in any way, but rather because they have not had appropriate educational experiences.
4. Too few practitioners have education in the research- or knowledge-creating process and are therefore unable to use findings that would be applicable to solving their problems.
5. Researchers too often write for and publish their findings in reports and journals that are not read by practitioners.
6. Practitioners too often fail to read research literature.
7. Coordinated and accessible dissemination systems for research findings have not been adequately developed.
8. Practitioners, but also often researchers, fail to use the dissemination systems available.

BRINGING THE WORLDS OF PRACTITIONERS AND RESEARCHERS TOGETHER

In this period of increasing demand for accountability and decreasing funds, it is time that researchers and practitioners reach an understanding about the synergistic relationship that should exist between them so that they can join together to solve critical problems in their fields. What follows are some suggestions as to how a base could be developed from which an improved understanding could be reached.

What Practitioners Can Do

First and foremost, all members of a field must be educated in appropriate knowledge production processes. Although it is not necessary that this education be in such depth that all practitioners are capable of undertaking knowledge production, it is necessary that they have sufficient knowledge of the appropriate processes to be able to translate on-the-job problems into appropriate problem statements and, further, that they be able to read the field's literature with sufficient understanding to determine its meaning and utility. It will not be sufficiently timely to simply require all who are now entering the field to take methodology courses while obtaining their basic education, although this should definitely be done. In order to reach a timely and effective understanding, present practitioners who do not feel comfortable with their basic knowledge of methodological processes must acknowledge their dis-ease and proceed to relieve themselves from it.

Undoubtedly, the most effective way for practitioners to learn the basics of methodological processes is to take courses; however, with an ability to extrapolate basic research process knowledge to the field's problems, practitioners can benefit from taking an introductory methods course offered in any related discipline. Such general research methods courses are readily available in community colleges, colleges, and universities. If it is not possible to enroll in a semester- or quarter-length course, a continuing education short course would be a useful beginning point for practitioners. Head librarians might also engage in in-house staff development projects through bringing an instructor in research methods/problem solving to the library to highlight the importance of the acquisition of this knowledge.

Becoming familiar with methodological processes is one of the best investments that practitioners can make for both themselves and their profession. Acquisition of knowledge production processes enhance the practitioner's self-image. Further, because research and researchers are generally held in high esteem throughout society, the value of the field to society will also be enhanced. A community of practitioners with greater sophistication about knowledge production processes would do much to alleviate the problems that beset communication between the field's researchers and practitioners; they would be better able to identify researchable problems, and researchers would be more likely to turn to them for problem identification. The language barrier between the two groups would be lowered, and practitioners would be better able to evaluate the utility of the research literature.

What Researchers Can Do

The burden of lowering the communications barrier between researchers and practitioners does not lie solely with the practitioner. Researchers need to publish their research findings in journals that are read by the practitioners for whom the results would be most useful. They should write articles using clear direct language. Unfortunately researchers seem to write most often for the benefit of other researchers and do so chiefly because they are more interested in and dependent upon having their work evaluated by their research peers rather than their practitioner colleagues. It is difficult to "blame" researchers for doing this because most often those doing research are employed by institutions that reward them through promotions or tenure based upon peer recognition rather than colleague acceptance. The journals in which the researcher must publish in order to gain peer recognition are not those to which practitioners generally turn.

It would do a great deal to lower the communications barrier between researchers and practitioners if researchers would also write versions of their results for journals aimed primarily toward practitioners. It would not be difficult for them to do so using common, shared language, referring readers of the practitioner-focused version of their findings to the research-focused version so as to assuage any doubts they might have regarding the constraints that a practitioner-focused version would undoubtedly face. But most researchers, it should be understood, would prefer to (and should) spend their time moving on to new research projects that will add depth or scope to the field's knowledge base. They should not spend their time writing a practitioner-focused report of research that has already been completed and published for the research community. If a larger number of practitioners became knowledgeable about the research process, they would more often be involved in the research process from its inception. They could become partners on research teams, and one of their major responsibilities could be the writing of practitioner-focused versions of research reports.

Although there is never a panacea for all the ills that beset a field, certainly an increase in the research sophistication of the practitioner community would go a long way towards improving the usefulness of the research that is undertaken, delivering to practitioners results of more useful research.

PUBLISHING RESEARCH RESULTS

As was stated at the outset of this essay, it is critically important to publish research results. To reiterate: publication allows others to have access to results in a reaccessible package. Although it is also important to communicate with practitioners through presenting papers at professional meetings, it is only through publication that access can take place at a time determined useful by the practitioner. Publication assures, to the extent possible, that research results are reaccessible. Publication allows for the evaluation of results and, further, allows those who would find it useful to repeat research in a different setting or using a different methodology to do so. Although academia-based researchers usually publish their research results, too often practice-based researchers do not. They often seem to believe that their research is only of interest in their own setting or will have little utility in another setting. Although this may indeed be true, it is preferable to let an editor or reviewers of submitted manuscripts make that judgment.

Although it is true that a portion of the research that is published is not used by practitioners either because it is really not of use or is unintelligible (unintelligible either because of the way in which it is written or because practitioners lack the basic skills necessary to be able to understand it), the results of much significant research are available. Yet, much useful research is not easily available because it is only accessible by searching several indexing and abstracting tools. The field of education has several well-developed dissemination networks: the National Diffusion Network, the Research and Development Exchange, and the Educational Resources Information Center (ERIC). Practitioners in library and information studies must begin to demand more easily available access to research results in our field.

DISSEMINATION OF FINDINGS

There are three basic types of dissemination: one way, two way, and audience based. (These three types are based upon material in *Increasing the Impact of Social Innovations Funded by Grantmaking Organizations* [Lindquist, n.d.].)

Type I Diffusion

Definition
One-way communication—disseminator *to* audience. Examples are publications and speeches. Generally one-shot approaches. Material centered.

To Be Effective
Be clear. Be simple. Use logic and evidence. Gear to a specific audience. Make it visible. Encourage safe trials. Be flexible. Use a variety of methods and messages.

Skills Required
Knowledge of the material being diffused; presentation ability.

Limitations
This approach informs but does not persuade. Unless the material is easy to communicate and the audience is ready, it will result in use by only a few. Most people need interaction over time with respected leaders to become convinced. In addition, the audience may not have implementation authority.

Type II Diffusion

Definition
Two-way communication—disseminator *with* audience. Examples are participative workshops and consultations. Includes linking agents and interaction networks.

To Be Effective
Seek credibility. Be actively available. Find and use friends. Be openly flexible. Train local linking agents. Create interaction networks. Keep group work numbers small.

Skills Required
Knowledge of the material; presentation ability; knowledge of alternatives to the material for solving the same problem; ability to facilitate information-sharing workshops; commitment to the material and openness to audience.

Limitations
Requires prolonged personal contact; may not provide sufficient impetus for local implementation.

Type III Diffusion

Definition
Audience centered. Disseminator facilitation of local adaptation. Goals are local development of innovations with existing research results as stimulants and guides to adapt, not adopt, and to increase local systems

problem-solving ability. Includes assessment of local needs; linking local audiences to one another; aiding collaborative formulation and decision making; aiding in preparation for implementation.

To Be Effective

Establish contact with decision-making authorities. Encourage and practice openness of both information and motives. Develop a leadership team. Collaborate with audience to create local ownership of result. Make involvement rewarding—intrinsic satisfactions and formal rewards. Seek valid and reliable information. Note benchmarks but keep at it.

Skills Required

Knowledge of material; presentation ability; linkage skills; ability to facilitate information sharing; commitment to material and openness to audience; and ability to use material in the context of local development and adaptation.

Limitations

Requires intensive facilitation of local planned change but probably is the only way to create impact in complex systems.

QUALITY OF DISSEMINATION

Communication and research results must be clear whether a presentation is oral (formal or informal) or written (formal or informal). The first consideration is answering the following questions (Hernon & McClure, 1990, p. 199):

- Who is the audience and what are their needs and expectations?
- Is the communication well prepared, credible with and understandable to that audience?

The second consideration is to decide how visuals will enhance the presentation.

Upon completion of either the paper or the outline upon which an oral presentation is to be based, or of a written report, journal, or book manuscript, one should go through the following checklist in order to identify areas that need additional clarification, simplification, or development (Hernon & McClure, 1990, p. 210):

1. Are the study components (e.g., the problem statement and objectives) clearly and concisely stated?
2. Have the objectives, hypotheses, and/or research questions been adequately addressed?

3. Are the findings, conclusions, and recommendations clearly stated and do they match the objectives, hypotheses, and/or research questions? Do the findings, conclusions, and recommendations appeal to the intended audience?
4. Where necessary are significant or potentially controversial statements supported by the literature?
5. Are there weaknesses in logic or mistakes in spelling or grammar?
6. Are concepts and technical words adequately explained?
7. Could a major point be better represented through a table or figure?
8. Are sentences repetitive, clearly expressed, and easy to read?
9. Is the report/article objective?
10. Does the report/article [sound good] or read well?
11. Does the title adequately describe the contents of the report?
12. Is the use of headings and subheadings consistent throughout the report?
13. Is each paragraph essential and in its proper place?
14. Does one paragraph flow naturally into the next?
15. Does the report/article contain contradictions?
16. Do sentences contain passive voice, wordy thoughts, and unnecessary words?
17. Is there consistent use of hyphens, spelling, and word capitalization?
18. Are references accurate and do the dates in the list of references match those presented in the text?
19. Are pages numbered correctly?
20. Are tables and figures correctly numbered?
21. Are quotations correct?
22. Is there any copyright problem associated with the quotation of text?
23. Are all references necessary?

It is also valuable to have *at least* one critical ear or eye go through the presentation or manuscript prior to its being presented or submitted to clients or editors.

CONCLUSION

How then is research useful in practical terms? Although the specific impact of research on decision making can seldom be documented, the awareness of research on the part of decision makers is a component of that amorphous attribute called "professional judgment." The practitioner's knowledge of research findings, along with experience, common sense, intuition, and familiarity with local traditions and politics, all play a role in decision making. Using research results in decision making is important for at least two reasons: First, many service-related decisions would undoubtedly be improved if the results of research were clearly delineated as one of the choice factors. Second, a more vigorous reliance on research results rather than on the more subjective elements of professional judgment would surely enhance the effectiveness of the field within its local institutional environment. It would clearly be in the best interests of practitioners if the findings of research could become a larger and *more visible* element in decision making.

In order to balance what is usually an overdependence on local, situational factors in decision making with research-based factors, research must be of dependable quality and capable of withstanding the critical scrutiny of the institutional officers and constituents to whom practitioners are accountable. For this reason, the most critical issues for users of research are those having to do with upgrading the quality and usefulness of research. Among these issues are the following (Hewitt, 1983, p. 131):

1. The need to develop and propagate standard, reproducible research designs specific to the problems of the profession.
2. The need to re-orient some segments of the professional research community to more useful approaches and methodologies.
3. The need for improved training in research design and methods in library schools, both to produce better qualified researchers and more critical and demanding consumers of research.
4. The need for effective orchestration of research efforts in order to create a coordinated approach to major research problems.
5. And finally, the need to acquire a stronger empirical base for understanding the interaction of research and practice in librarianship.

REFERENCES

Hernon, P., & McClure, C. R. (1990). *Evaluation and library decision making.* Norwood, NJ: Ablex.

Hewitt, J. A. (1983). The use of research. *Library Resources & Technical Services, 27*(2), 123-131.

Lindquist, J. (no date). *Increasing the impact of social innovations funded by grantmaking organizations.* Battle Creek, MI: W. K. Kellogg Foundation.

Schön, D. A. (1983). *The reflective practitioner: How professionals think in action.* New York: Basic Books.

ADDITIONAL REFERENCES

Bain, H. P., & Groseclose, J. R. (1979). The dissemination dilemma and a plan for uniting disseminators and practitioners. *Phi Delta Kappan, 61*(2), 101-103.

Etzioni, A. (1968). *The active society: A theory of societal and political processes.* New York: Free Press.

Griffith, B. C. (1991). Understanding science: Studies of communication and information. In C. L. Borgman (Ed.), *Scholarly communication and bibliometrics* (pp. 31-45). Newbury Park, CA: Sage Publications.

Johnson, J. M. (1984). Dissemination of information from home economics research. *Home Economics Research Journal, 12*(4), 470-480.

Lievrouw, L. A. (1990). Reconciling structure and process in the study of scholarly communication. In C. L. Borgman (Ed.), *Scholarly communication and bibliometrics* (pp. 59-69). Newbury Park, CA: Sage Publications.

McClure, C. R. (1991). Communicating applied library/information science research to decision makers: Some methodological considerations. In C. R. McClure & P. Hernon (Eds.), *Library and information science research: Perspectives and strategies for improvement* (pp. 253-266). Norwood, NJ: Ablex.

Pierce, S. J. (1990). Disciplinary work and interdisciplinary areas: Sociology and bibliometrics. In C. L. Borgman (Ed.), *Scholarly communication and bibliometrics* (pp. 46-58). Newbury Park, CA: Sage Publications.

Robbins, J. (1988). Communicating research in the information profession: An essay. In P. Elliott (Ed.), *Current research for the information profession 1987/88* (pp. a5-a15). London: The Library Association.

MARGARET MARY KIMMEL

Professor and Chair
Department of Library Science
School of Library and Information Science
University of Pittsburgh

Ivory Tower or Temple of Doom: Some Questions Concerning the Application of Research

ABSTRACT

The relationship between research and application is explored in the context of the delivery of information service to children and young people in schools and public libraries. The status of research in the field is discussed, and the use of interdisciplinary research is suggested. Finally, obstacles to the implementation of programs for young people are described.

INTRODUCTION

A recent episode of "Star Trek: The Next Generation" begins with Commander Geordie LaForge's excitement over the expected visit of the engineer who designed the new engines of the starship Enterprise. His excitement is enhanced by the fact that he had met the research engineer at a conference, and his admiration extends beyond engine design to the person of the researcher—he thinks she is lovely. On the other hand, when the designer arrives, she is not amused; Geordie has messed with her design. Poor Geordie is puzzled; he only tried to make the design work more effectively.

This episode led me to think about a number of issues related to the relationship between research and application, between researcher and applier, between clinical and theoretical approaches to questions

89

in our professional lives. I would like to explore some of these issues in the context where I find questions most challenging—the delivery of information services to children and young people in both schools and public libraries. Although there are significant administrative differences in the systems, some overriding issues are strikingly similar.

STATUS OF RESEARCH IN THE FIELD

Interest in what kind of research is being done—and not done— is always keen, at least among us academics whose health and well- being quite literally depend on it. To others, research results are often of marginal importance. A call to a very small sample of public library directors indicated that not one had used a research study as a basis for a decision in the past year. Why not? Answers ranged from "It's dull," to "Things move too quickly around here to translate what some esoteric study says to what I need to know today." Such attitudes might shock *us,* but I doubt that they would make the wider world gasp.

In spite of this attitude, there are three recent developments that have some potential for research. The first is the Treasure Mountain retreats in 1989 and 1991, which have gathered together groups of individuals interested in the research of issues related to school library media centers and their staff. This is a small nucleus of people, and results are hard to estimate after so short a time.

Most of the work so far consists of reviews of the literature—as reasonable a place to begin as any (Woolls, 1990). Yet some of these reviews demonstrate a remarkable lack of understanding of the breadth of an issue. For instance, Loertscher offers a review of literature in reading and school library media centers and makes assertions about the reading process that is not documented in his review of research. He states that "over-the-summer (holiday or break) reading helps retain learning" (Loertscher, 1990, p. 60) and neglects to cite studies by Locke (1988) or Heyns (1978). In fact, much of the review fails to take into account any of the work done in literacy or emergent literacy by such noted scholars as Teale and Sulzby (1986); Heath (1983); Heath, Mangiola, Schecter, and Hull (1991); or Smith (1988).

The second notable addition to the potential for research in this area is the effort to collect baseline data on the service. For many years, this special service has not been broken out of data regularly collected by state or federal agencies. The National Center for Education Statistics (NCES) has attempted to remedy this situation by collecting national, baseline data on library service. Two studies, one for children's services (NCES, 1990) and one for service to young adults (NCES, 1988), looked at staffing patterns, hours open, use by children, young adults, care providers and other adults, and attempted to identify resources and services provided. It included analysis of cooperation with schools and preschool or daycare centers. Data were collected for individual library buildings rather than for systems, and budget figures were based on book budgets and the percent of that budget allocated to children and young adult resources.

As with any survey of this type, however, there are some limitations. As the final report notes, "American public libraries are tremendously diverse, both in the services they offer and in the communities they serve. Patronage in the libraries in this nationally representative sample ranged from 7 patrons per week to 34,315 patrons per week, with a mean of 1,007 patrons per week" (NCES, 1990, p. xiii). That is a pretty high range of diversity and makes generalizations difficult.

Garland (1990) has added to information about the availability of statistics. Her work, recently distributed to all those teaching in the area of children's and young adult services or school media programs in American Library Association (ALA) accredited schools, identifies the data collected by each of the fifty states. This information is valuable, but it too demonstrates the problems with using these figures for comparative purposes, because there is no consistent pattern of collection. For instance, twelve states collect no information at all about the children's materials or services or staff in public libraries. In the area of school media services, twenty states collect no information at all; two states collect budget information only; four states are in the process of developing some data; and one did not even respond.

A third example in the research of the past several years is part of the Public Library Development Program, the *Output Measures for Children's Services in Public Libraries* (Walter, 1992). Although it is difficult to categorize the work as research per se, the *Output Measures* suggests a method for individual libraries or systems to analyze and evaluate the service provided to children and young people.

So what do these three projects indicate about new research ventures? Both the NCES surveys and the Garland compilation do provide a starting point for measurement and evaluation. The picture is certainly not complete, but the Federal-State Cooperative System for Public Library Data (FSCS) may finally begin to include data on service to children and young adults. The project, which is supported by both the National Commission on Libraries and Information Science (NCLIS) and NCES, may be what is needed to make the statistical comparisons possible. The work of Dr. Mary Jo Lynch should be recognized in encouraging these efforts.

On the other hand, the existence of such baseline data does not necessarily indicate more meaningful research. As a first step to systematic collection of data, which may be able to give a more comprehensive picture of the service provided over time, these projects are significant events. Research on a national level, however, is fragmented by the nature of the service it attempts to measure. Most of the research about the "system" is operational, not theoretical, in nature. This statistical approach looks at what *is* and does not explore the nature of the system or provide for analysis of what focus the service should have.

These efforts have focused on the area of data collection, but examination of other areas indicates that research topics are scattered, researchers isolated, and results rarely reported beyond the dissertation committee or a rather dry journal report. In other words, they are dull. Reviews of the literature by Shontz (1982), Edmonds (1987), or Fitzgibbons (1990) refer again and again to the lack of a theoretical framework. There would appear to be more research in just sheer numbers on the educational end of the spectrum, but it too fails to accumulate evidence in any one area that is significant enough to draw attention beyond the confines of the ALA American Association of School Librarians (AASL).

Another consideration relates to the number of people interested in the area. There is often little critical mass within the individual departments or schools to allow collaborative efforts—or even brainstorming. There is virtually no teamwork and few instances of cooperation across territorial lines. One effort to conduct a study of the service to young people in four states has been on the table for more than three years. The researchers, all with fine minds, powerful understanding, and good intentions, have not had the dedicated time or the burning need to get the project off the ground. One has been promoted to full professor, one to associate, one to chair of a department, and one has changed jobs (and state), all without the necessity of doing more than talking about the study.

USE OF INTERDISCIPLINARY RESEARCH

If studies are not being conducted in the field, are there those from outside that could affect service delivery? There is some evidence that documents how other agencies have worked at providing service to children and young people in a viable way. Schorr's *Within Our Reach: Breaking the Cycle of Disadvantage* (1989) provides an example of what can be done. By analyzing reports and longitudinal studies that followed children's development from earliest infancy to adulthood, and by talking with researchers and people who work on front lines with families in trouble, Schorr studied those projects that successfully helped children and their families. She discovered much was already known about the delivery of service as well as what that service should be. Schorr says, "I was dismayed at how little of this knowledge was being utilized to change the prospects for children growing up in the shadows" (Schorr, 1989, p. xviii). It may be that this type of analysis, grounded in the anecdotal, descriptive literature that comprises most of our reporting would be a step forward in plotting directions for service.

And consider, for a moment, one scholar's work, which could have a major influence on the development of service. Shirley Brice Heath has studied the way in which communities interact with the young in preparing the children for school. In a three-year ethnographic study in the Carolina Piedmont region, Heath (1983) found that families prepared their children for the ways of the world in a manner that was usually nurturing and loving. Such preparation, however, did not always give the child a background necessary to participate in a complicated social scheme that demanded abstract as well as concrete understanding of ideas related to literacy and literate behavior. In other words, parents who did not value books and reading did not share them automatically with their children. Heath's work has demonstrated that the sharing of stories through reading aloud to young children is *the* significant factor in preparing the children for school. All parents want their children to succeed. If sharing book reading is the link to literacy, and reading aloud is the key, it is obvious that the library—school and public—unlocks that paralysis we call illiteracy and makes the librarian a major force in the literacy process.

Have we been involved in the application of this rather remarkable study? The answer is yes, to a degree, but usually in scattered "pilot programs," funded on soft money and eliminated from the scene when the funds run out. There are a few exceptions, and Pittsburgh's Beginning with Books is one of them. It is a project that began with soft money in 1983 to distribute books and tips about reading aloud to families in well-baby clinics in Allegheny County. The program now works with more than 38 agencies and has several other components, one of which is a three-year, half million dollar project to work with care providers in homes and daycare centers on the value of, how to, and what to read aloud. Soft money, yes, but the program is an affiliate of the Carnegie Library of Pittsburgh, which covers not only overhead but one full-time staff salary and other assistance.

Yet Heath's work is not widely known or quoted in the library press. Although she has participated in literacy conferences and even an annual meeting of ALA, the work of this MacArthur scholar does not serve as a basis for our planning and development of service. Although her studies provide overwhelming evidence that the emphasis on reader guidance and work with both children and adults is significant, they are ignored by planners and managers.

In our efforts to prove the impact of service with the accumulation of numbers, we too often ignore the theoretical framework. For instance, in a recent issue of *Public Libraries,* a study reviewing the cost-effectiveness of service to children in the Montgomery County Public Library (MD) is presented (Mielke, 1991). One finding of the study was that a children's literature discussion group (of adults) was too time consuming for staff to justify in terms of adults served. Only an average of seven people attended on a regular basis. The program was cut in favor of a program for those who needed English as a second language. On the one hand, it is an honorable management strategy to take a hard look at matching time and effort against attendance. On the other, the problem of the effectiveness may be more related to focus and design. Certainly there is much evidence that working with the adults who care for and about children may be *the* most cost-effective way in dealing with not only literacy-related impact, but the service as a whole. Did the planners consider the evidence of research and the experience of the Hennipen County Public Library (MN) and the Orlando (FL) Public Library, for instance? In these two libraries, major service efforts to deliver service to children are aimed at adults working *with* children, teachers, scout leaders, parents, Sunday school workers, or others. Evidence indicates that placing information about books, videos, puppets, stories—i.e., the resources of the library—in the hands of adults who care for children would provide the most direct and intensive and cost-effective delivery possible.

CONCLUSIONS

Evidence is accumulating slowly that documents the impact of service to young people. There are, however, some significant obstacles in the way. We know, for instance, that the service to children and young people must be provided early, offered consistently and continuously, and that we have effective models of how to operate. Implementation of such a program warrants careful thought and direction. It requires planning by enlightened managers and that may mean changing the behavior of those who deliver the service. We know the impact of reading aloud, the motivation of story. But as one reading specialist said to me, "It is too easy. We've spent millions on machines and studies on different ways of reaching these kids. Now you say, give a teacher a book and tell him to read to the class? The Board (of Education) would have my head."

In another district, Title I families were targeted for reading programs. Parents and kindergarten children were gathered together in the early evening, with the children being read to and playing while the parents focused on what and how to read to the children. A journal was kept of what happened from week to week, and indeed documented over and over again the results. Kids read better; parents read more; stress in the family was lessened. There was one major problem, however. The school library media director refused to let the groups meet in schools libraries; they would disarray the place, and school librarians would have to straighten things the next day. The planners compromised; what if the instructors—who were reading teachers in the system— checked out materials from the school libraries so that parents could get extra books to take home? No, that simply would not do. What if books were lost? What if they were damaged? What if the books were stolen? The director produced a statement from the school system's legal department forbidding the circulation of library materials for the project.

And there are examples from the public library sector, too. We are slow to move and slower to innovate. Children's services programs are cut as budgets are reduced. But the research evidence shows, time and time again, that we provoke more problems down the line every time we lose or cut a program for children and their families now. "Excellence costs. But in the long run, mediocrity costs more" (National Commission on Excellence in Education, 1983).

Research is most successfully applied, it seems to me, when it is applied with passion. Research can inspire, if it is creative, the confidence in the decision you as provider need to make when faced with barriers of scorn or skepticism. But it must be applied by those who know of it; it must be sold to those who hold the funds and the power of implementation. It is not easy. If I could wave a magic wand and say, based on research, here is the fact that will impress all the public officials, from mayor and council to local principal, to fund this service that will break the cycle of illiteracy in the United States of America, I would do it. But research itself is not magic; it is a tool. It is the people who wave the wand who provide the magic.

REFERENCES

Edmonds, M. L. (1987). From superstition to science: The role of research in strengthening public library service to children. *Library Trends, 35*(3), 509-520.

Fitzgibbons, S. (1990). Research on library services for children and young adults: Implications for practice. In K. Haycock (Ed.), *Program advocacy: Power, publicity, and the teacher-librarian* (pp. 7-18). Englewood, CO: Libraries Unlimited.

Garland, K. (1990). Unpublished report.

Heath, S. B. (1983). *Ways with words: Language, life, and work in communities and classrooms.* Cambridge: Cambridge University Press.

Heath, S. B.; Mangiola, L.; Schecter, S. R.; & Hull, G. A. (Eds.). (1991). *Children of promise: Literate activitiy in linguistically and culturally diverse classrooms.* Washington, DC: NEA Professional Library, National Education Association.

Heyns, B. (1978). *Summer learning and the effect of schooling.* New York: Academic Press.

Locke, J. L. (1988). *The effectiveness of summer reading programs in public libraries in the United States.* Unpublished doctoral dissertation, University of Pittsburgh, Pittsburgh, PA.

Loertscher, D. V. (1990). Reading research and school library media programs. In B. Woolls (Ed.), *The research of school library media centers: Papers of the Treasure Mountain research retreat, Park City, Utah, October 17-18, 1989* (pp. 49-63). Castle Rock, CO: Hi Willow Research and Publishing.

Mielke, L. R. (1991). Sermon on the amount: Costing outchildren's services. *Public Libraries, 30*(5), 279-282.

National Center for Education Statistics. (1988). *Services and resources for young adults in public libraries.* Washington, DC: U.S. Department of Education, Office of Educational Research and Improvement.

National Center for Education Statistics. (1990). *Services and resources for children in public libraries, 1988-89.* Washington, DC: U.S. Department of Education, Office of Educational Research and Improvement.

National Commission on Excellence in Education. (1983). *An open letter to the American people: A nation at risk: The imperative for educational reform.* Washington, DC: U.S. Government Printing Office.

Schorr, L. B. (1989). *Within our reach: Breaking the cycle of disadvantage.* New York: Doubleday.

Shontz, M. L. (1982). Selected research related to children's and young adult services in public libraries. *Top of the News, 38*(2), 125-142.

Smith, F. (1988). *Joining the literacy club: Further essays into education.* Portsmouth, NH: Heinemann.

Teale, W. H., & Sulzby, E. (Eds.). (1986). *Emergent literacy: Writing and reading.* Norwood, NJ: Ablex.

Walter, V. (1992). *Output measures for children's services in public libraries.* Chicago: American Library Association.

Woolls, B. (Ed.). (1990). *Research of school library media centers: Papers of the Treasure Mountain research retreat, Park City, Utah, October 17-18, 1989.* Castle Rock, CO: Hi Willow Research and Publishing.

J. R. BRADLEY

Assistant Professor
Graduate School of Library and Information Science
University of Illinois at Urbana-Champaign

Choosing Research Methodologies Appropriate to Your Research Focus

ABSTRACT

This paper considers the generic activities involved in research and some issues that underlie whatever specific methodologies the investigator selects. A general definition of research (or empirical inquiry as it is generally termed in the paper), broad enough to encompass multiple research traditions and methodologies, is developed: systematic connection of observation of the empirical world with abstraction about the empirical world in ways that consciously seek to identify and control for bias and thus provide the most complete view that is relevant to the purposes and focus of the inquiry. Five activities necessary in the process of empirical inquiry are discussed: (a) finding a focus, (b) describing the problem to be investigated, (c) selecting the phenomena in the empirical world to observe, (d) observing the phenomena, and (e) analyzing and interpreting the observations. Each activity is described, major issues are considered, and, where appropriate, alternative approaches represented by deductive and inductive research traditions are presented.

INTRODUCTION

The task in this paper is to consider what the library practitioner who undertakes a research project needs to know about research methodologies. There are obviously a great many issues involved with choosing research methodologies and with carrying them out appropriately. Texts on research methodologies within the field of library and information science (e.g., Busha & Harter, 1980; Mellon, 1990) and numerous texts treating research in the social sciences in general (e.g., Miller, 1991; Kidder & Judd, 1986; Kerlinger, 1986; Dubin, 1978; Patton, 1990; Strauss, 1987) provide excellent descriptions of and instruction in various methods or traditions of empirical investigation. (*The Handbook of Research Design and Social Measurement* by Delbert Miller [1991] is a comprehensive handbook that provides an excellent starting place for a wide variety of research issues. The capsule descriptions of techniques are useful, and each description is accompanied by a short but generally very useful bibliography to carry you further into the topic.) An individual investigator must choose the methods of empirical inquiry that are best suited to his or her specific problem and purposes. The process of designing and implementing a good research project is, in essence, putting together and following a plan that consciously matches methodology with the particular characteristics of what the investigator wants to know.

The research guides cited above, and other books and articles from their bibliographies, will provide you with detailed discussions of procedures and techniques for using specific methodologies. This paper approaches the topic from a slightly different perspective by considering the generic activities involved in empirical inquiry and some issues that underlie whatever specific methodologies you select.

The term "research" means different things to different investigators, often connoting primarily the particular methodologies or research traditions that each uses. In this paper, I am following Paul Diesing's usage of the phrase, research tradition, to refer loosely to research that shares assumptions, definitions of problems, and techniques or procedures for addressing them (Diesing, 1991). The notion that research processes can be grouped together based on a common set of assumptions and ideas of what constitute problems and how best to research them without bias is frequently discussed under the label "paradigm," loosely following Thomas Kuhn's notion of a paradigm (Kuhn, 1970). Kuhn's revised concept of a paradigm, developed with reference to research in the sciences, refers to an exemplar or a specific procedure for solving problems. His usage seems more specific than the notion referred to here, and therefore I have preferred the term "research tradition." To sidestep the confusion of multiple definitions of what constitutes "research," this paper will generally prefer the phrase "empirical inquiry." A definition of this process will be developed now.

Kidder and Judd (1986) describe research as systematic observation conducted to support or modify theories and hypotheses about social behavior (p. 21). From this and similar definitions in other texts, three elements can be identified: (a) abstractions in various forms, including words for phenomena and descriptions of relationships among phenomena; (b) observation, or the activity of observing phenomena in the empirical world; and (c) the systematic development of links between observation and abstraction, or between the observed phenomena and abstract accounts.

Kidder and Judd go on to contrast research as a way of knowing with ordinary knowing. In the ordinary way of knowing, people construct abstract explanations, called hypotheses by Kidder and Judd, about why the things that they see around them occur; in other words, the ordinary way of knowing involves connecting the phenomena in the empirical world with abstract ideas about the phenomena. Kidder and Judd suggest that the most important difference between ordinary knowing and research lies in the systematic search for biases in the research process (pp. 4-21).

Bias in empirical inquiry is a concept that can be interpreted numerous ways, often depending on one's research tradition, from being synonymous with error to referring to a particular slant, perspective, or point of view on a subject. Bias, in this paper, will be defined very broadly as a partial view or incomplete view. In the normal course of work life, librarians, like professionals in any setting, tend to develop knowledge about the settings around them in ways that resemble what Kidder and Judd describe as ordinary knowing. The papers in these proceedings address the use of empirical inquiry by library practitioners as a way of approaching their work—as a way of knowing. Extrapolating from Kidder and Judd above, an important part of making the transition from ordinary knowing to knowing through empirical inquiry is the systematic search for the biases in the process through which you come to conclusions.

In this paper, the process of empirical inquiry will be defined as the systematic connection of observation of the empirical world with abstraction about the empirical world in ways that consciously seek to identify and control for bias and thus provide the most complete view that is relevant to the purposes and focus of the inquiry.

ACTIVITIES IN THE PROCESS OF EMPIRICAL INQUIRY

For the purposes of this discussion, the process of empirical inquiry will be divided into five activities: (a) finding a focus, (b) describing the problem to be investigated, (c) selecting the phenomena in the empirical world to observe, (d) observing the phenomena, and (e) analyzing and interpreting the observations. In research practice, these activities overlap and are recursive to a greater or lesser degree.

The identification of separate activities is in many ways artificial, but it serves the purpose of focusing attention on one aspect of the research process at a time.

Finding a Focus

Much empirical inquiry that library practitioners wish to undertake starts with a question or problem that arises in a specific library, frequently in the context of decisions to be made or action taken. Often investigators begin with some idea of their purpose in undertaking inquiry, as, for example, a project to determine the need for additional reference desk staffing to cope with increased demand for assistance related to CD-ROMs and the automated catalog. This first conception of the purpose for the inquiry often shapes the initial formulation of its focus.

The initial formulation of a problem often arises out of concrete circumstances, so it may be very specific. Alternatively, the first formulation may be quite broad. Whatever the level of specificity, the first formulation usually views the problem from a specific perspective. A perspective, used in this sense, is a set of ideas about what elements in the situation are important. A perspective, or way of looking at an issue, focuses attention on certain factors and precludes looking at other factors in a situation. In other words, the perspective in a sense "predefines" what phenomena or elements are worth looking at. Your initial perspective at the beginning of a project may well end up being the one you want to use; however, focusing your attention on specific elements before you have surveyed a broad range of factors runs the risk of ignoring other important and influential elements in a situation.

As a first step in finding your focus, then, it is useful to consider your field of interest broadly, from multiple perspectives. This process of attempting to look at problems from a variety of perspectives, and thus considering as many relevant factors in a situation as possible, has been described by Bolman and Deal (1991), in the context of making management decisions, as "reframing." To illustrate the process of reframing, or viewing a situation from multiple perspectives, let's look at a specific hypothetical situation. Suppose that, as the head of an academic reference department, you have observed that the introduction of six new CD-ROM stations over the past year has created a chaotic situation where the reference librarians cannot respond adequately to patron need. Librarians are complaining that they are spending too much time fixing machines and not enough time answering reference questions; support staff are being asked to help out and that is taking time away from their work and causing other frictions; and patrons are complaining that they can't get help, that the machines aren't working and that often no one can fix them, and that not all the staff are friendly and helpful when problems occur.

You decide that, before taking action, you will undertake a process of empirical inquiry to understand more fully the situation you face. In terms of this paper, you decide to take systematic, preplanned steps to link observations of the world around you with abstractions that explain that world, in ways that will be subject to as little bias as possible.

Initially, you may see this problem as one of staff scheduling, providing more librarians at peak usage time; so the focus of inquiry might be on establishing patterns of demand. Alternatively, you might see the problem as one of job definition and perhaps specialization: who is supposed to be doing what jobs in relation to the computers. A focus here might be to establish what tasks are actually being performed, or are needed. Or perhaps you may focus on issues of appropriate levels of service, expectations of the users, or appropriate types of training and instruction. Another possible way of looking at the problem might concern the technophobia or technophoria of both staff and users. Or, perhaps you may consider it simply a budgetary problem: more reference librarians are needed, and the problem becomes how to demonstrate to resource allocators that more resources are needed.

Note that each one of these formulations focuses on certain elements and excludes others. Inquiry that was driven by each of these perspectives would collect data on certain aspects of the situation and not others.

"Reframing," or looking at situations in new ways, can be quite difficult. The more recalcitrant or chronic the problem—the more resistant it has been to previous analysis and solution—the more difficult, and the more important, it might be to consider alternative perspectives in an effort to generate more factors to consider.

What are some concrete ways to foster "reframing" in exploring a problem? One approach is to involve people who are affected in various ways by the problem to participate in the problem exploration, such as people with administrative responsibility, librarians, support staff members, student or other part-time workers, users, and administrators outside the library. Michael Patton (1982), in *Practical Evaluation*, discusses ways to involve all stakeholders in formulating the questions that will be asked. Not only will you get more heads working on the problem, but since different groups of stakeholders view problems differently, more perspectives, and more factors, may arise.

Reviewing the library literature, and especially the literature of other disciplines, can be a source of fresh perspectives. The literature can provide discussions from other perspectives, formal theoretical treatments of problems, and empirical studies. Identifying a theoretical treatment of a problem that seems to address the relevant issues is often a useful way of providing a framework for inquiry. The same issues of perspective apply in evaluating whether a particular theory addresses all relevant issues that you feel you need to address. In the CD-ROM example, the literature on the introduction of new technology into the workplace may suggest interesting factors to consider in analyzing the problem. Different theories suggest different factors, however. As an example, theories differ in the extent to which they address gender issues in technology. Bolman and Deal (1991) suggest also becoming familiar with theoretical perspectives that are somewhat different from the entrenched ways of analyzing situations. Examples of less familiar perspectives are what Bolman and Deal define as the political perspective and the symbolic or cultural perspective. Perspectives that look at gender issues might also be considered in this category. (For an introduction to gender issues in research, try *Feminist Methods in Social Research,* by Shulamit Reinharz [1992].) Identifying colleagues who have had success in coping with similar problems or who are trying innovative solutions is another strategy for broadening perspectives.

It may be useful to think of the process of finding your focus as drawing boundaries that will specify the phenomena of interest to you and something about their relationships. The problem becomes one of finding the best balance for your purposes. Boundaries that are too widely drawn may result in more complexity than can be adequately studied. Boundaries that are too narrowly drawn may exclude complexity that is necessary to an adequate understanding of the situation. Any solution necessarily involves a compromise between what you would like to know and what you feel you can adequately investigate. You may find it useful to try to draw the boundaries as narrowly as you can and still retain the complexity that you feel is necessary to serve your purposes. Again, involving stakeholders in helping define these boundaries is one way of insuring that multiple perspectives relevant to the context of the issue in a real-life situation are included in your inquiry.

Once you are satisfied that you have identified as many perspectives, and as many potentially relevant factors as possible, you can begin to reconstruct your description of the problem.

Describing the Problem under Investigation

Once you have defined the focus for your inquiry, you are ready to move to a more specific description of the problem you will investigate. That description of the problem will be the framework that guides the rest of your activity. We will look at two issues involved in specifying the framework: (a) the abstractions that you use to describe the elements of the framework, and (b) the specific form your description of the framework takes.

Your formulation of the framework for your inquiry will consist of abstract statements identifying phenomena and frequently some explicit or implied assertion of the relationships among phenomena. Examples relating to the CD-ROM example can show the wide range of possible abstract descriptions of phenomena: "activities relating to CD-ROM," "professional reference librarians," "library staff," "clerical, technical, and professional tasks related to CD-ROMs," "users' requests for help with CD-ROMs," "willingness to provide help," "positive attitudes toward computers," "willingness to instruct in search strategies," "instruction in search strategies," and "library users."

Brinberg and McGrath (1985) make a distinction between phenomena or elements that arise from the substantive, or empirical, world and those that arise from the conceptual world. For example, abstractions such as "professional reference librarian," "library staff," and "library users" come from the substantive world of libraries. Elements such as "willingness to provide help" come from the conceptual domain and are often called constructs. Other examples of frequently used constructs are "job satisfaction" or "motivation."

It is very useful to be able to define for yourself the meaning of the abstractions that appear in your problem description, particularly the more abstract constructs. These constructs may come from theories or the literature and may have a history of varied definitions, as does the construct of "job satisfaction." The wording you choose for your abstractions and the meanings that the words have for you have important consequences for your inquiry because they drive the activities that follow.

Another issue involved in the description of the problem you are investigating involves the specificity of your formulation. Descriptions of problems can take a number of forms and can vary in the specificity with which they pin down the abstractions of interest and the relations among them. Several possible descriptive formulations include a narrative, a research question or a series of questions, and specific explanatory statements or hypotheses. The narrative is useful for pinning down the perspective or conceptual framework that you have settled on, even when you move on to develop research questions or specific hypotheses. If you are using formal theory to guide your inquiry, you may wish to write a concise description of your specific situation, using the abstractions and constructs of the theory. For example, if your investigation focused on the extent to which Shoshana Zuboff's concept of "informating" was occurring in libraries, you would not only want to define the concept of "informating" but also to describe informating in the context of your specific situation (Zuboff, 1988). That description serves as the framework for your investigation of informating.

It is also useful when developing the narrative to note the perspectives and phenomena that you have excluded in drawing your boundaries. These are issues that you will not be investigating directly. At the end of the project, when you are interpreting the results, you may find it helpful to reflect on what you did not study as a way of further illuminating what you did study.

How specific should your formulation of your framework for inquiry be? Will you be guided by a general research question, or will you develop specific hypotheses that will guide your observation of the empirical world? It may be helpful to think of formulations of focus on a continuum. At one end are very general abstractions that draw very loose boundaries around the phenomena and their relationships that you will look at. In the CD-ROM example, a research question that falls at the general end of the continuum might be the following: What activities do reference librarians perform in relation to CD-ROM? Note that the general nature of the abstraction "activities relating to CD-ROM" draws very loose boundaries within which observations will be conducted.

A slightly more focused question might specify types of activities: What clerical, technical, and professional tasks are performed by library staff members? In specifying types of activities, you have introduced more specific constructs. You will need to define these constructs carefully so that you are clear about what you mean by "clerical" or "professional" tasks. Note that the act of definition itself can often illuminate potential difficulties in your research framework. Suppose, for example, that you define "professional tasks" as those done by professional librarians. If the purpose of your research is to identify different types of tasks that reference librarians are performing, and one of your categories is defined as the tasks librarians perform, then you have involved yourself in circular reasoning and demonstrated the need for either a specific list of professional tasks or specific criteria— other than the performer—by which to assess which tasks are professional.

At the other end of the continuum are very specific abstract statements that draw very close boundaries by specifying relationships among abstractions. Your inquiry, then, is focused on seeking evidence to support or disconfirm the existence of these relationships. Examples of several specific hypotheses coming out of the CD-ROM problem might be the following: (a) professional reference librarians are performing clerical, technical, and professional tasks related to the CD-ROM searching systems; (b) among professional reference librarians, knowledge related to computers is associated with willingness to provide whatever level of help with CD-ROM the user asks for; (c) among professional reference librarians, positive attitudes toward computers are associated with willingness to instruct users in search strategies.

Virtually every empirical investigation—regardless of the tradition or procedures—includes specific statements of relationships among abstractions based on some systematic observation of the empirical world. Research traditions vary, however, as to the stage in the process where these statements of relationship—which can be called hypotheses—come. One group of research traditions—which can be loosely termed the deductive traditions—creates the specific statements of relationships (the hypotheses) before entering the empirical world to observe. Observation of the empirical world is then structured to support or disconfirm specifically formulated relationships.

Another group of research traditions—which can be loosely labeled inductive traditions—develops statements about relationships from observation of the empirical world. The statements of relationships are developed and assessed in the process of observation rather than formulated in advance to guide investigation.

A number of considerations can help you decide whether deductive or inductive approaches are most useful for a specific inquiry. Consider whether you feel your present understanding of the topic is sufficiently complete that you will not be excluding factors of central interest by focusing only on certain relationships. Ask yourself, for example, if your abstract or theoretical narrative describes what you feel are the relevant elements and their relationships.

Consider, also, whether the set of specific relationships you are looking at can be meaningfully isolated from the larger context. Often combining deductive and inductive methodologies is a way to confirm or disconfirm specific relationships while also providing a broader context for interpreting the total situation. A last consideration involves whether or not you wish to make use of statistical methodologies to make inferences about a broader population based on the data from the sample under investigation. Deductive traditions have well-established procedures for extending your conclusions beyond the group from which you have collected data, and specific hypothesis formulation figures prominently in those procedures.

Selecting the Phenomena to Observe

The description of the problem to be investigated provides an abstract framework for your observations of the empirical world.

Empirical inquiry represents a systematic or structured linking of abstraction and observation, so it is necessary to specify the procedures or means by which you plan to look for your abstractions in the empirical world. This step—of connecting abstractions and statements of relationships among them to real-life exemplars—involves specifying what the abstractions mean in specific terms, including how you will recognize them in the real-life world.

The strength of the match between your abstractions and the empirical phenomena you choose to observe is the crux of good inquiry. To control bias, investigators must observe phenomena that represent as closely as possible the abstractions talked about in their problem statement. This concept—the close link between the abstract constructs and specific representations (including the way they are defined, identified, and observed) in the empirical world—is labeled as correspondence validity by Brinberg and McGrath (1985) in *Validity and the Research Process,* a comprehensive text that pulls together notions of validity from many different traditions in research. The term "construct validity" is often used in deductive traditions to refer to the idea of the fit between the abstraction or construct and what is being measured.

It is useful to talk about four potential weaknesses that can occur in linking abstract descriptions (of any specificity, from research question to specific hypothesis) with observations of the empirical world. These problems exist whether the link comes before observation or during it.

The first potential weakness is that the observations incorporate phenomena or relationships other than, or in addition to, those specified in the abstractions; in other words, the empirical phenomena are actually more complex than your abstract description of it recognizes. For example, people who hold MLS degrees in libraries frequently have management responsibilities or have different status in the organization from people who do not hold the library degree. The MLS degree thus measures people who are in the professional class of "librarians," but it also may be measuring people who have certain functional or status roles in the library. The potential implication for your inquiry is that the factors that are shaping the outcomes that interest you are not related to the MLS but are, in fact, related to functional or status roles.

Another weakness is that what you plan to observe is more simple or encompasses less than the ideas in your abstract framework. In this case, the empirical data may miss important elements of the situation that are implied by your abstractions, either because your observations were too restricted or because they did not tap the essence of the problem you were studying. Suppose that you are studying reference transactions, and you decide that you are interested in the use of a certain body of abstract reference knowledge to solve certain kinds of problems. This statement of your construct of interest implies a definition of "professional librarian" as one who knows and uses certain abstract knowledge. If you choose to represent this construct in your inquiry by individuals holding MLS degrees and working in reference departments, you may not be zeroing in as specifically as possible on the essence of your construct—use of abstract knowledge. Measurement by the MLS may exclude those who have the appropriate abstract knowledge but do not have the degree, and it may lump together widely varying types or levels of abstract knowledge acquired during an MLS but say nothing specifically about reference knowledge. In other words, the MLS may not be a sufficiently precise indicator of the abstraction that really interests you—abstract reference knowledge.

The third potential weakness is that the phenomena being observed change, perhaps systematically, as a result of conditions that the investigator does not take into account; in other words, the phenomena being observed are not stable across time and situations. Another way of thinking about this problem is that there may be changes in conditions affecting what you are observing that are not apparent to you but that affect what you observe. Consider, for example, a situation where you specify that you will observe instances of the abstract concept of "reference librarian" by identifying persons with an MLS who are scheduled on the reference desk. Suppose also that the week you chose to observe MLS-degreed staff who were scheduled on the reference desk was also the week of a national conference on bibliographic instruction, and so librarians from other parts of the library were filling in for the regular reference librarians. Or suppose that during the semester you conduct your inquiry, several reference librarians are on leave, or new staff without experience are being trained. This example, although somewhat simplistic, illustrates differences in phenomena that you have not controlled and that may result in measuring unequivalent phenomena and not recognizing it.

A special case of the problem of observation of variables occurs in relation to the knowledge and attitudes of humans. Can we assume that an individual holds a set of unitary, unconflicted, and stable ideas in relation to complex subjects? Might the circumstances in which questions are asked and answered call up different aspects of complex patterns of belief? How do we deal with the possibility that humans will forget or fail to recognize the relevance of an idea, opinion, or attitude to a question? To what extent are the ideas, attitudes, and knowledge that an individual articulates produced as a result of the combination of factors at the time the question was asked? Do people act based on consciously articulated rationales, or do they construct them afterwards? To put some of these considerations in a concrete context: If a librarian is asked on multiple occasions to articulate his or her views about the appropriate balance between teaching patrons how to use complex reference sources and actually consulting the sources for the patron, will these views be the same, or reasonably so? These are complex issues, and are raised here merely to introduce the problem of consistency of human response.

A last potential weakness is that the "instruments" or "tools" that gather the data introduce variation that will produce observations that are not stable across time and situations. These instruments can be human or nonhuman. When we ask respondents to give us facts, we are, in essence, using them as measurement instruments. For example, if we ask a library director to provide us with the characteristics of a library staff, we are using her as an instrument to measure the staff. Many factors, including mental definitions used, time and care taken in gathering data, extent of verification, concentration, and motivation may cause the description of the same phenomena to vary. Anyone who has worked with library statistics will probably testify to the difficulty of providing the same measurements in the same way over time, even when definitions are provided.

The correspondences between observation and abstraction are never complete. Investigators are constantly in the position of having to *act as if* there were correspondence where, in fact, it is only partial. This behavior is frequently called making simplifying assumptions. It is an inevitable part of inquiry, but it is also an inevitable source of bias, and the investigator must take the responsibility for assessing the effect of these assumptions on the results and minimizing it as much as possible.

The deductive and the inductive approaches were introduced earlier in connection with the stage at which hypotheses are created. These two approaches provide useful ways of looking at alternative strategies for linking abstractions and observations.

Deductive research traditions involve the progressive narrowing of focus from theoretical formulations specifying constructs and their relationships to specific units or entities representing the abstractions— and often called variables—that will be measured. This narrowing process is frequently called "operationalizing." It is founded on the assumption of operationalism, which takes as a given that constructs can be observed and measured. Kidder and Judd (1986, pp. 18, 40-41) provide useful definitions and discussion of this process, moving from the abstract constructs to concrete representations of those constructs, termed the variables. An operational definition is a series of steps or procedures identifying the way in which the variable is to be measured. It is important here to point out that measurement need not be limited to quantification. Measurement, in this sense, can be represented by both words and numbers, as long as the procedures for measuring the variables are articulated and could be followed by other investigators to replicate measuring the abstraction in the same way.

Choosing the variables that will represent, or stand for, your abstractions and then specifying the procedures by which you will measure those variables are among the most important decisions you make in the deductive process, since what you measure provides you with the evidence that you will use to draw your conclusions. A rationale behind deductive methods is that predetermination of what you will look at focuses your inquiry and makes it precise, allowing you to include only what you want to include and exclude other factors. The extent that you are able to meet this ideal always remains problematic. In predetermining your constructs, variables, and operational definitions, you introduce potential sources of bias.

Subjecting your own abstractions and operational definitions to the scrutiny outlined above will help you understand the conceptual leaps that are built into your own framework for inquiry. You can use statistical tools to help point out where some gaps between abstraction and operationalization may exist (see discussions of validity and reliability in Kidder and Judd and other texts). Even with numerical indicators pointing toward potential problems, you as investigator need to understand the nature of problems and the effects on your results. Conceptual analysis of this kind can also alert you to situations where you may wish to approach linking constructs and observation in other ways, including using the inductive approach.

Whereas deductive approaches specify the concrete phenomena they will study before they gather data, inductive approaches reverse the order of these activities. Inductive approaches gather information about concrete phenomena in the empirical world, and then from these data— through the process of analysis—abstractions are developed. For this reason, the discussion of specifying the connection between abstraction and observation will be treated in more detail in the discussion of step five—analysis and interpretation.

Under what circumstances might you, as an investigator, consider inductive approaches to linking abstractions with concrete phenomena? Three lines of reasoning will be presented that provide slightly different although somewhat overlapping rationales for choosing to conduct inquiry following inductive approaches. The first rationale uses terms such as discovery or exploration and covers situations where the investigator wants to get a sense of what the relevant or influential phenomena are. Perhaps the investigator is not ready to settle on particular constructs or hypotheses. Perhaps the investigator feels that the variables that have been investigated in past work have not satisfactorily explained the situation and wishes to explore other approaches. Discovery or exploratory use of inductive methods may lead to the specification of particular constructs and variables that can generate models and hypotheses. Brinberg and McGrath (1985) call this activity the prestudy or generative phase "in which a researcher develops, clarifies, and refines the elements and relations" (p. 26) of the area of interest. Strauss and Glaser (1967) have described a similar activity as "grounded theory," and Eisenhardt (1989) describes the process of developing abstractions from the ground up in specific, procedural terms, making her article a good place to start exploring this tradition.

In our CD-ROM example, using the constructs of clerical, technical, and professional tasks, an investigator may decide, perhaps after struggling with criteria for defining these tasks as they relate to CD-ROMs, that these categories are problematic. He or she may choose instead to collect data about as many tasks connected with CD-ROMs as possible and then analyze the data to determine the relevant abstract ways of describing tasks. He or she may also feel that this approach will suggest relationships between either types of staff and activities or between activities and staff attitudes, or between other factors that he or she does not yet anticipate.

A second rationale for using inductive approaches goes beyond exploration, although the notion of discovering relationships by analyzing a broad spectrum of data is certainly included. This rationale is founded on the assumption that it is difficult for the investigator to identify, from an outside perspective, the terms that are meaningful to those actually in a specific situation. An underlying assumption is that people act on the basis of what objects and situations mean to them, and that this meaning arises from the person, acting within the situation. In this view, operational definitions formulated by deductive investigators may or may not coincide with the way the participants themselves define phenomena. Therefore, although participants in deductive inquiry may provide data within the categories, that data will not reflect distinctions that the participants themselves would make. And since these distinctions form some of the basis for participants' actions, the deductive investigator is missing important data relating to behavior.

Applying this rationale to the CD-ROM example would lead us to want to know how the staff members themselves perceive the tasks related to CD-ROM. This rationale would argue that the investigator should not predefine the tasks for the respondents but instead should design data collection to allow the understandings and attitudes the staff have toward these tasks to be captured. The distinction being made here can be illustrated by analogy to traditional ways of gathering reference statistics in libraries. These statistics are typically gathered in categories such as "short" or "ready" reference, extended reference, or directional questions. Many librarians working with such statistics have wondered how much homogeneity there is in the responses in each category. Does every librarian have the same definition of a short reference question or a directional question? And if not, does lumping them all together hide some useful distinctions? Inquiry that focuses on understanding how participants view situations themselves comes from several different research traditions, including ethnographic research (for example, see Spradley [1980]) and naturalistic inquiry (see, for example, Lincoln & Guba [1985] or Mellon [1990]).

A third rationale for inductive approaches stresses the importance of viewing complex phenomena like social and organizational situations from a holistic point of view. This reasoning assumes that focusing on a limited number of variables at a time distorts the total picture and ignores the complexity of many interrelated parts. The reasoning further argues that since the whole is more than the sum of the parts, the parts change, or lose meaning, when they are viewed in isolation. Although gathering a broad spectrum of data does not in itself ensure that complexity can be captured or understood, such an approach, its proponents argue, provides a better view than an approach that dissects the whole into parts or variables. This view tends to stress integrated interpretation that reasons from concrete empirical data, including the understandings of participants, and develops an interpretation which it then checks against additional data or additional situations.

In the preceding section, we have examined some broad strategies for approaching the link between abstraction and concrete phenomena. Both deductive and inductive approaches have strengths that suit them for certain kinds of problems, and both introduce sources of biases. You, as investigator, have the task of choosing the strategy that best fits your purposes, a strategy that will err in ways that are *least* likely to compromise your results.

Observing the Empirical World

Whatever approach you choose to link abstraction to phenomena in the empirical world, you will need to design strategies to collect data on those phenomena. If you have followed deductive strategies, you have already specified a set of procedures, or parameters, that will guide you in data collection. However, you will still need to develop and use your data-gathering instrument, and in doing so, you will be again narrowing or limiting the data that you will be gathering.

If you have followed inductive strategies, you have developed your focus, and in addition, you will need a more or less specific plan to guide data collection. The details of your plan will be shaped by your focus and by how much you wish to prespecify your data collection efforts. You will need to consider questions such as the following: From whom will you gather data? Over what period of time? On what topics or subjects? What types of data? Under what circumstances will you gather data? How will you record responses (e.g., from memory, with tape recorders, on forms)? What questions will you ask? Will you ask the same questions of everybody? Will you use prespecified wording?

Specification of the way you will observe the empirical world is an activity common to both deductive and inductive traditions, and similar problems arise. To illustrate some of these choices, we return again to the issue of the CD-ROMs: Suppose that you have decided to collect data on the activities of reference staff in relation to CD-ROMs. Who will you ask to provide you with this information? You can ask the reference staff themselves what activities they perform; you can ask someone else in the situation, the head of Public Services for example, or perhaps the support staff members or the patrons; you can look for what is called "trace" evidence, artifacts that indicate activity has gone on (in this example, calls to service people; ribbons and paper used; searches performed would all be trace evidence); or you, as a investigator, can observe, either as an outsider or as a participant. Each of these sources of information will provide a different perspective on the activities involving CD-ROMs that the reference staff perform, and it can be argued that each provides a partial picture. Each also has a characteristic bias, resulting from the perspective each information source brings to the question. Because many data-gathering techniques rely on self-report data, it will be considered briefly here.

Self-report data (and data provided by any other individual including the investigator as observer) will reflect the way that individual views the situation. The key question for the investigator is whether that view is biased, or different from other views, in a way that is relevant to the research question. Suppose, for example, the reference librarian reports an activity as "taught search strategy to patron using PsychInfo." As a investigator, you might ask yourself whether all participants providing information about CD-ROM activity will mean the same thing by those words. Or, to look at the other side of the problem, will every participant who explains boolean logic to a patron record that activity on the form using the same words?

Suppose another participant explaining boolean logic to a patron had described the activity as "explained commands to patron." Would you as researcher recognize the same underlying activity, or would you conclude that the two different descriptions referred to two different actions? If you feel that the distinctions reflected here will not obscure phenomena that are important for your research question, then the issue of participants' perspective may not be important in this instance. If, however, you feel that the underlying distinctions behind these characterizations of activities are important to keep clear, then you need to give more thought to the issue of perspective. One compromise frequently encountered is to gather information from several perspectives. For example, the investigator might ask the reference staff to keep a diary of activities, perhaps using a random alarm device. The investigator could also observe sessions in which the staff kept these logs and compare his or her assessment of activities with the assessments of the librarians. If the investigator found high consistency among all participants, then he or she can have confidence that multiple perspectives are not unduly influencing data gathering. If, on the other hand, the investigator discovers widely differing descriptions of the same activity, perhaps among staff members, that difference might then become the focus of investigation.

We have been talking about observations that have been gathered in verbal form. Collecting data in words provides you with great variety in data and introduces many complications in aggregating and describing that data. It also introduces complications, as we have seen, in understanding what phenomena those words referred to and in comparing phenomena. When drawing conclusions—interpreting verbal data—further complications arise concerning multiple meanings.

It is important to note, however, that gathering data in categories or as numerical responses on a scale does not avoid the issues of multiple meanings inherent in gathering verbal data. The initial problem of aggregation is somewhat simplified, since you can count categories and use descriptive statistics to provide numerical summaries. However, the problem of multiple meanings has been submerged rather than erased. You still need to be reasonably certain that all respondents had reasonably similar understandings of the categories. The analogy of library statistics is again useful here. Does everyone have the same definition of a reference or a directional question? What are the implications for the aggregated totals if individuals have interpreted the categories differently? And if variation of understanding of the categories is possible or probable, what are the implications for the similarity of the interpretations of the aggregated totals by the investigator and the consumers of the results?

The key question for you as investigator is this: Will multiple meanings that participants, investigators, and readers have result in misunderstanding of important issues embedded in the problem you are investigating? If so, a combination of measurement techniques may be needed to provide both aggregation and sufficient clarity for

Applying Research to Practice

interpretation. Structured and unstructured interviews, surveys, observation, analysis of documents, and performance of tasks can be used in both deductive and inductive data gathering. The way these tools will be used may differ, depending on the specificity with which data is being gathered, and each approach has a wealth of literature specifying appropriate techniques. The investigator's task is to choose and adapt the tools that best fit the purposes of the specific research question.

Analysis and Interpretation of Data

Analysis and interpretation of the finding of empirical inquiry is more or less dependent on decisions made in earlier phases of inquiry, although the extent of that dependency varies in different traditions of research. For deductive strategies, analysis and interpretation theoretically come after the data have been collected. Techniques for data analysis, specifically numerical and statistical techniques, are well worked out and discussed at length in the literature and are too voluminous and complex to be discussed here (see Miller [1991] for an introduction to these topics and use his bibliographies for follow-up).

In inductive strategies, the link between abstraction and concrete empirical phenomena is developed through a reiterative process of collecting data from the empirical world, developing tentative explanations or abstractions that make sense of the data, and then returning to the empirical world to assess the abstractions in light of concrete phenomena. The process of testing the abstractions (or hypotheses) proceeds by looking for disconfirming or negative evidence. That evidence can be found in data collected from the initial situations, but most inductive traditions incorporate an active search for disconfirming evidence guided by reasoning about what disconfirming evidence might look like and where it might be found.

Suppose, for example, that you, as an inductive investigator, were investigating the activities of library staff in relation to CD-ROM activities and gathered interview and observational data through a variety of methods over the course of several weeks. Let us further suppose that preliminary analysis of that data led you to speculate that people with positive attitudes toward computers provided much more help to users than those with negative attitudes. As a first step in exploring this explanation, you might go back either to your data, or preferably to the empirical world itself, looking specifically for people with less than positive attitudes toward computers and analyzing their patterns of helping users.

Suppose, further, that you then began to see what you thought were patterns within the patterns you had identified as positive and negative attitudes. At first, you might see these patterns represented only by one person, as for example, the librarian who criticized automation as making the staff dependent on machines, while at the same time praising the ability of the computer to do keyword subject searching. As you examined the responses of more people, you might begin to group together similar expressions of views about computers and perhaps eventually suggest categories of attitudes along different dimensions than positive and negative. You might then return to the empirical world to look for observations that did not seem to fit your new categories.

In inductive approaches, the interpretations—or the development of abstractions—perform the function of aggregation in deductive approaches; they simplify the diversity of individual cases by providing descriptive abstractions, often in the form of categories or constructs. In other words, interpretation creates the link between the observation and the abstraction by defining it. The four potential weaknesses involved in linking abstraction and observation apply at this stage. In deductive traditions, numerical processes (tests for validity and reliability) can help somewhat in alerting the investigator to these problems. In inductive approaches, and in the interpretation by which the deductive investigator extends analysis of categories to further abstractions that they represent, there are fewer cut-and-dried indicators. The primary inductive tool is to assess each abstraction against as much data from a wide variety of situations—often systematically selected— in order to detect anomalies of fit. Techniques in inductive traditions are proliferating in the current wave of interest in these methods, providing both procedures and examples of ways to minimize bias in the matching of abstraction and observation (see, for example, Miles & Huberman [1984] or Strauss [1987]).

CONCLUSION

In summary, this paper has proceeded under the assumption that all empirical inquiry—observation systematically linked with abstraction—introduces bias of one sort or another. Although it is the function of method to systematize inquiry and thus reduce potential bias, the method itself is also a source of bias. Investigators have the responsibility of understanding the sources of potential bias introduced by the methods that they use in all activities of the process of empirical inquiry and of using that understanding in the formulation of the conclusions that they eventually present as the result of their inquiry.

REFERENCES

Bolman, L. G., & Deal, T. E. (1991). *Reframing organizations: Artistry, choice, and leadership*. San Francisco, CA: Jossey-Bass.

Brinberg, D., & McGrath, J. E. (1985). *Validity and the research process*. Beverly Hills, CA: Sage Publications.

Busha, C. H., & Harter, S. P. (1980). *Research methods in librarianship: Techniques and interpretation*. New York: Academic Press.

Diesing, P. (1991). *How does social science work: Reflections on practice*. Pittsburgh, PA: University of Pittsburgh Press.

Dubin, R. (1978). *Theory building* (rev. ed.). New York: Free Press.

Eisenhardt, K. M. (1989). Building theories from case study research. *Academy of Management Review, 14*(4), 532-550.

Kerlinger, F. N. (1986). *Foundations of behavioral research* (3rd ed.). New York: Holt, Rinehart and Winston.

Kidder, L. H., & Judd, C. M. (1986). *Research methods in social relations* (5th ed.). New York: Holt, Rinehart and Winston.

Kuhn, T. S. (1970). *The structure of scientific revolutions* (2nd ed.). Chicago: University of Chicago Press.

Mellon, C. A. (1990). *Naturalistic inquiry for library science: Methods and applications for research, evaluation, and teaching*. New York: Greenwood Press.

Lincoln, Y. S., & Guba, E. G. (1985). *Naturalistic inquiry*. Beverly Hills, CA: Sage Publications.

Miles, M. B., & Huberman, A. M. (1984). *Qualitative data analysis*. Beverly Hills, CA: Sage Publications.

Miller, D. C. (1991). *Handbook of research design and social measurement* (5th ed.). Newbury Park, CA: Sage Publications.

Patton, M. Q. (1982). *Practical evaluation*. Beverly Hills, CA: Sage Publications.

Patton, M. Q. (1990). *Qualitative evaluation and research methods* (2nd ed.). Newbury Park, CA: Sage Publications.

Reinharz, S. (1992). *Feminist methods in social research*. Oxford: Oxford University Press.

Spradley, J. P. (1980). *Participant observation*. New York: Holt, Rinehart and Winston.

Strauss, A. L. (1987). *Qualitative analysis for social scientists*. Cambridge: Cambridge University Press.

Strauss, A. L., & Glaser, B. G. (1967). *The discovery of grounded theory: Strategies for qualitative research*. New York: Aldine de Gruyter.

Zuboff, S. (1988). *In the age of the smart machine: The future of work and power*. New York: Basic Books.

BLAISE CRONIN

Dean and Professor
School of Library and Information Science
Indiana University
Bloomington, Indiana

When is a Problem a Research Problem?

ABSTRACT

Various definitions of and approaches to research and research problems are explored with numerous examples given. Guiding criteria for applied research are also discussed, along with potential pitfalls, the role of intuition in the process, and the qualities that are needed to make a good researcher.

PROLOGUE

"The Brains Trust" was one of the earliest and most popular TV shows broadcast by the BBC. It featured a panel of highbrows and academics who fielded questions from the general public on every conceivable subject. The questions were not especially abstruse, more like the kinds of questions posed by my three-year-old daughter: seemingly simple, but ultimately confounding. Prominent among the pioneering panelists was the late philosopher, C. E. M. Joad, who, if my memory serves me right, unfailingly began his reply to each question with the phrase, "Well, it all depends what you mean by . . . ." Such, indeed, was my internalized reaction on receiving the title of the present paper. It is not one I would have chosen, and the question is certainly not one I have ever posed or been posed. Problems, large and small, domestic and professional, are everyday features of my life, and research (funded and independent, basic and applied) is something I have been doing for the last fifteen or so years. But I haven't given a great deal of thought to the nature of problems, at least not since reading Bertrand Russell's (1959) *The Problems of Philosophy* as a freshman, and my theorizing about research has tended to focus on issues of style, methodology, and management rather than root definitions.

PROBLEM OR OPPORTUNITY?

There is a perfectly simple reason why this has been so. Since I began researching in this field, I have never had to look for a research problem: ideas for research tumble naturally out of workplace experiences, literature immersion, and routine intellectual trading. The things I do, read, hear, and say provide the inspiration for my personal research. Since this conference is concerned with practitioner aspects of research, let me illustrate: In 1978 I was employed as an entry-level professional in a small/medium-sized public library in London. The library was sited in an area with (a) high ethnic diversity, (b) poor quality housing stock, (c) multiple social deprivation, and (d) low income levels. The library was keen to reach out to nonusers in the local community. There are two ways of looking at this: The library's objective was to reach those who could not be reached, or the library's problem was not being able to reach those it wanted. Objective, problem, challenge, opportunity. The word is largely irrelevant. At the time, I was interested in the marketing of library services, so I designed an experiment using five different direct mailing shots to compare the relative effectiveness of the five different packages/approaches (Cronin, 1980). In the longer term, my goal was to identify predictors of positive response to advertising campaigns of this kind.

A presurvey of the target population used construct clustering techniques to evaluate different kinds of promotional materials and guide the design process. The five experimental groups were painstakingly matched in terms of (a) type of accommodation, (b) social class, and (c) proximity to library. New library registrations from the family units of all those included in the five groups were monitored for four weeks to gauge the relative effectiveness of each promotional package. Less than 1 percent of those mailed joined the library over the four-week period. Hardly an experimental success, but, with hindsight, hardly surprising. Nonetheless, a good example of how we can learn from negative results.

As a piece of practitioner-conceived and conducted research, the study was not without charm and ingenuity. And it was low cost. It highlighted the inappropriateness of direct mail advertising for a certain kind of nonuser population. But it was driven by a curiosity to see whether the factors that influence nonuse could be modulated by a particular form of targeted advertising. Nonuse may, for some, be a problem, but as I look back, I realize that my motivation was curiosity rather than problem resolution. I did not conceptualize my study in terms of a research problem, though if someone had referred to it in such a manner I would not have batted an eye.

COLD WATER . . . COLD FUSION

"The deep secrets of Loch Ness are to be laid bare in what is claimed will be the first full and credible scientific exploration of its depths" ran the July 19, 1991, story in the *Glasgow Herald*. A funding package of almost $3.5 million is being assembled by the Natural History Museum (London) and the Freshwater Biological Association to "determine how the loch works and how it supports its plant and animal populations." Project Urquhart, as the investigation will be known, acknowledges "that there have been a number of interesting observations at the loch which have yet to be explained" and that it "is highly likely that species new to science will be discovered." As one who has had an interesting, if fleeting, observation while on the loch, and who thus runs the risk of being dismissed as a crank, it is a relief to find that the apparatus of scholarly research is finally being marshalled in a serious and determined effort to separate fact from fancy.

Over the years, there have been many attempts to pin down the elusive Nessie, some of which have produced interesting, if ultimately inconclusive, results. The Loch Ness "mystery" is researchable and certainly seems to provide a challenge for a variety of researchers, some more sophisticated and serious-minded than others. There is a hypothesis; there exists a variety of evidence, from folklore to home movie footage; there are many eye witness accounts, albeit of variable reliability; there are investigative techniques (from naturalistic to experimental) that could be used to determine the nature and scale of subaquatic life in the loch; and there is a range of technologies that can be wheeled into action (e.g., sophisticated sonar testing devices and image-enhancing systems to facilitate tracking and analysis). In that sense, Loch Ness has many of the features of a research problem. For some, there is a desire to know unequivocally whether Nessie exists or not; for many others, the answer, affirmative or negative, will sound the death knell for magic realism in the Highlands.

During 1989 and 1990, cold fushion was a hot issue. Pons and Fleischmann's high-profile media announcement of their "discovery" (via TV newscasts and the pages of the world's financial press) broke the unwritten rules of the scientific community. In the race to be first, Pons and Fleischmann cut corners, sidestepped the scholarly press, and withheld information from their peers. The cold fusion saga shows what happens when commercial considerations (the potential payoffs from patentable discoveries in cold fusion would have been massive, as both the University and State Government of Utah fully realized) collide with the essentially cautious and consensus-seeking nature of the scientific communication process (Close, 1990).

This deviant behavior provoked physics labs around the world to put their claims to the test. Replication proved impossible, and the duo fled the limelight. Because cold fusion offers the prospect of cheap, safe, and abundant energy, Pons and Fleischmann's claims generated feverish and unprecedented speculation inside and outside the scientific community. Cold fusion became a research problem. And the mainstream scientific community responded with a battery of corroboration-seeking research.

PUZZLES AND DIFFICULTIES

And so to root definitions. There are at least two kinds of problems: puzzles and difficulties. Puzzles are things for which there are solutions (e.g., a crossword, conundrum, jigsaw, Rubik's cube); difficulties are things we have to cope with, but for which convincing or lasting explanations should not necessarily be expected (e.g., explaining apparent regularities in underlying macroeconomic behavior, dealing with the depletion of the earth's natural resources). We may not solve a puzzle for any one of a number of reasons (e.g., failure to grasp a clue; we misread the rules of the game), but in theory a puzzle is soluble. Not necessarily so with difficulties. Difficulties exercise our ingenuity; they are also relative. What is difficult for me may not be difficult for you. And the nature of difficulties may be redefined or better understood as a result of research (e.g., corn circles, quarks), but the fundamental problems (e.g., the nature of matter and of the universe) remain as challenging and resistant to full explanation as ever. Problems, then, can have final or potential solutions. The Loch Ness monster is more of a puzzle, while cold fusion remains, despite repeated failures to replicate the results, a difficulty.

In library and information science research, we have puzzles and difficulties. Reasons for collection nonuse, user failure at the shelf or at the catalog, and communication breakdowns in the reference negotiation process are puzzles for which in specific instances we should be able to come up with plausible explanations and solutions. Trying to define what we mean by information, or determine what constitutes the basic unit of information, or put a monetary-equivalent value on information are difficulties—they are the hardy annuals of research in this field, and the best we can hope for is a greater appreciation of the complexities and nuances of the problem domain. Even the simplest library use survey is hamstrung by the difficulty of defining use in a meaningful manner: Surrogate measures (e.g., document exposure time) tell us nothing about the nature of the interaction between user and text; nothing about the amount of intellectual capital (if any) that was transferred; nothing about the degree of cognitive enrichment. The lack of a basic metric of information means that much of our research, and assumptions about the value of information interventions, rest upon questionable premises and approximate measures. Until now, research in our field has virtually ignored the motivational triggers that influence an individual's decision to use or not to use a particular quantum or parcel of information.

FIVE CONDITIONS

So back to the original question: "When is a problem a research problem?"—the wording of which seems to imply a need for more formalism and semantic precision than the Loch Ness and cold fusion cases provide. Sociologists of science have analyzed the ways in, and reasons for, which scientists select particular problems for research (Gieryn, 1978):

> *Problem choice* is defined as the decision by an individual scientist to carry out a program of research on a related set of problems, or more simply, in a problem area. . . . *Problem area* is defined as the accepted knowledge and recognized questions associated with a substantive object of study or with an instrumentational means of inquiry. A problem area is made up of a number of related though discrete problems, and a number of related problem areas are said to make up a specialty. (p. 97)

This kind of definition begs our question: It is as if scientists merely have to dip their hand into a pork barrel and pluck out a problem topic from a predetermined set, safe in the knowledge that such problems are "substantive" or susceptible to "instrumentational means of inquiry." For a brief moment after Pons and Fleischmann's announcement, funds flowed into cold fusion research. Once the bubble burst, the funds dried up: Cold fusion was in effect ejected from the pork barrel, as the scientific establishment reasserted its control over its research agenda. The establishment's reaction can be viewed as either a perfectly natural self-correcting mechanism or as an exclusionary strategy. Ortega y Gasset (1960) would, I suspect, favor the latter interpretation:

> All the individual sciences begin by marking off for themselves a bit of the Universe, by limiting their problem, which, once limited, ceases in part to be a problem . . . they start by knowing, or believing that they know,

> the most important aspect of it in advance. Their task is reduced to investigating the interior structure of its object, its fine innermost texture, we might say its histology. (pp. 61, 77)

The question could perhaps be paraphrased as: "What conditions have to obtain for a problem to have research problem status?" Consider then the following five generic conditions: pragmatism, instrumentality, reliability, credibility, and allocation. These are offered as a tentative rather than a definitive listing. In the case of pragmatism, the following conditions have to be satisfied:

- Curiosity is stimulated. ("Why is it that . . . what would happen if . . .?")
- The answer is not to be found in the literature. ("We have the question, but not the answer.")
- Conventional wisdom is defeated. ("Beats me.")
- Research funds are available (the cart before the horse approach).

All of these can apply as much to fundamental as to applied research: Curiosity may be the driver of a basic research program (e.g., defining the nature or value of information) or the trigger for a piece of amateur problem-solving research (how do we make local business more aware of library services; how can stock utilization be increased?).

The second condition, instrumentality, is triggered when

- an issue is tractable.

Research is thus defined as that which is researchable, and a research problem is one that enables the apparatus of systematic investigation to be mobilized in order to probe and to analyze data/subjects/phenomena. This, of course, is a circular definition, but if the parties involved dispute what constitutes admissible evidence or procedure, the circle can be broken. The Logical Positivists, for example, would not admit any kind of metaphysical speculation. For them, there could be no God, therefore there could be no problem. And if there is not a problem, there is no need for research.

A problem (e.g., a problem of morals or ethical behavior) can exist independently of results or of research methods: The status of a problem is not dependent upon the state of the art in research. For the members of the Vienna Circle, a problem may be a pseudoproblem, while for others (like Ortega y Gasset) it may simply be a problem for which the answer does not yet (or may never) exist. There are problems in science and in the social sciences for which adequate tools and reliability measures are lacking (e.g., the definition and measurement of human intelligence), but the problems remain problems.

However, in big science, little science, and parascience, problems are only deemed to have been solved when the results can be verified.

Science, broadly defined, has its rules that must be observed. The quality and admissibility of evidence and the means whereby it was derived matter a great deal. Whether we are talking about a proportionately stratified sample of cancer sufferers with a matched control group in the context of a NIH-sponsored (National Institutes of Health) study or a local survey of randomly selected library patrons in a busy shopping mall, users of the resultant research are entitled to know the assumptions, survey methods, and confidence limits employed. None of the conditions listed below has anything to do with the status of a problem, but they will have a bearing upon the perceived status of the results arising from the investigation of the problem. Reliability (and legitimacy in the eyes of many peers) will only have been achieved when

- results can be reproduced (unlike those of Pons and Fleischmann);
- results can be generalized or reasonable extrapolation made (as with basic informetric laws [Bookstein, 1990a, 1990b]);
- methods can be applied in other contexts (portability);
- resultant models have predictive power (e.g., Zweizig's [1973] analysis of predictors of library use/nonuse).

Credibility is another dimension that merits consideration. If our lawyer, doctor, or realtor is confronted with a problem in the professional domain, we have certain expectations that he/she will apply his/her forensic or technical skills in a systematic way to resolve that problem (e.g., the Center for Disease Control's Guidelines for Health Care Workers "encourage research to identify modifications for medical, surgical and dental procedures and develop equipment to reduce the risk of injuries to workers that might result in exposure of patients"). Here, of course, we are generally talking about quite different kinds of problems and research from those characteristic of the world of science. Professionalism creates a certain set of assumptions and expectations, which, in my view, includes the ability and willingness to conduct research and to solve problems. The condition of credibility is thus activated when

- perceived professional status creates the expectation among client groups that problems can be resolved by the application of appropriate research tools.

In other words, both the public and funding bodies are entitled to expect that professionally qualified librarians would have a research capability and a commitment to improving their services through focused investigation and experimentation, typically via problem solving or developmental research initiatives.

There are many occasions when trade-offs have to be made: A doctor may be faced with a choice between saving the child's or the mother's life; the librarian may have to choose between extended weekend opening hours and subsidized online services for the local business community. The trade-offs will not always be binary, but may involve an array of variables. In such cases, it may be necessary to carry out complex conjoint analysis to arrive at a weighted assessment of outcomes and implications. Research will therefore be necessitated when

- trade-offs are required (more of A and less of B, or vice versa?);
- questions regarding allocative inefficiencies are raised (what return on investment/yield is being generated?).

DEFINITIONS

But perhaps the problem is not so much with the word "problem," as with the term "research." The latter has acquired certain connotations (rigor, repeatability, measurement, etc.) and is powerfully associated with scientism in the popular mind. But this need not be the case. Overholser's (1986) definition, with its distinction between probable and probative, is a helpful corrective to this kind of myopia:

> Research is a far broader concept than science. Like science, it must be careful, systematic, insightful, persistent. But unlike science it need not be precise nor based on a theoretical construct, nor need it be subject to proof. Its findings need only be probable not necessarily probative. (p. RC-10)

And it is by no means a lone view. Patton (1986) offers an essentially qualitative definition of inference and extrapolation:

> Unlike the usual meaning of the term 'generalization', an extrapolation clearly connotes that one has gone beyond the narrow confines of the data to think about other applications of the findings. Extrapolations are modest speculations on the likely applicability of findings to other situations under similar, but not identical, conditions. (p. 206)

For the library practitioner (at whom my remarks are addressed), this is reassuring stuff. Findings need only be "probable" and extrapolations are categorized as "modest speculations," which in many working environments will be perfectly adequate to ensure that the results of research can be translated into actionable outcomes.

Let me illustrate not with a library case study, but by briefly describing an analysis of the strategic information needs of a Fortune 500 corporation's sales and marketing division. Our brief was open-ended: We were invited to define our research agenda. Basically, we investigated how a large manufacturing company supported the technical, market, and product information needs of its sales and marketing headquarters personnel and of its nationwide salesforce. Information was gathered through on-site observation of facilities, technologies, and information resources, and through interviews with senior and middle management and members of the salesforce. Convenience rather than representativeness was the criterion for selecting interviewees. We also drew upon a mass of background information on the company and its mainline competitors in order to provide contextualization.

What emerged, in a nutshell, was the centrality of field intelligence; intelligence that was unstructured, unvalidated, hot, speculative, and short-lived, and which was routinely gathered by members of the 250-strong salesforce. Our principal recommendations centered on the creation of a marketing knowledge base, which would pull together field intelligence on other players, products, technologies, key accounts, competitor pricing strategies, and third-party vendors, and permit this street-level information and intelligence to be integrated with other corporate information.

The study overthrew some of our safe assumptions about the importance of traditional information tools, sources, and resources in the context of a highly competitive and dynamic manufacturing environment. It highlighted the importance of social exchange, networking, and the leverage effect of distributed salesforce intelligence. In subsequent work for the company, we conducted a qualitative analysis of the impact of laptop computers on salesforce productivity (Cronin & Davenport, 1990). The study was to be two-part: part one predicting likely impacts and benefits; part two matching outcomes against benefits expected. For a variety of reasons the follow-up study could not be completed, but the insights that emerged from the exploratory phase (e.g., the longer term implications for space planning, property management, and relocation decisions) forced us to rethink the set of measures (hard and soft) that could be used to assess the downstream impact of support tools, such as laptop computers and cellular phones, on workforce attitudes, behaviors, and performance.

The conclusion to be drawn from all of this is that there is not (and probably does not need to be) a definitive answer to the question "When is a problem a research problem?" A more productive approach may be to consider how research (rather than problems) can be classified, and the following categorization is therefore suggested as a means of structuring essentially preliminary (and practicable) research ideas.

Contexts

Is the focal issue political, technical, managerial, scholarly, organizational, or personal in nature? It is important to be clear, as the answer will influence the style, conduct, and likely outcomes of the research. For example, a field-based survey of library nonuse among ethnic minorities will require a different style and approach from a systems audit in the technical services department of a major research library.

The Problem

Here there is a set of epistemological questions to be addressed: What is knowable? What do you need to know? How do you know when you know? What is the nature of knowledge in the problem domain? What are the chances of the problem being solved successfully? For instance, studies that attempt to measure the value or downstream effects of information will need to consider these kinds of questions.

Purpose

What are you planning/hoping to do with the results of your research? Will it be possible to apply the results? How will they be used? In what form must the results be gathered so that they have value-in-use? What, for instance, is the rationale for monitoring traffic flow through service points if the ability and willingness to reschedule personnel or opening hours are absent? What is the point of bibliometrically analyzing the use made of a journal collection, if, for political reasons, weeding and justifiable cancellations cannot subsequently be implemented?

Techniques

Which research methods and techniques (e.g., naturalistic, historical, action, ethnographic, experimental, content analysis) are most suited to the problem at hand? What combination of approaches would be most potent? What special capabilities will be required? How amenable is the problem to conventional or traditional lines of inquiry? Are the techniques commensurate with the problem? What particular sensitivities need to be taken into account? For example, a survey of OPAC use could combine audit trailing with direct observation and structured interviewing. An evaluation of scholarly performance in a research university might collocate weighted publication data and citation counts with peer review and receipt of honors and awards (the partial converging indicators approach), rather than rely upon a single measure. But a word of caution is called for:

> One should beware of researchers who collect research methods like others collect stamps and who tend to regard each project as an opportunity to add another method to their collection. (Moore, 1987, p. 10)

Validity

Validity can be of various kinds (e.g., construct, instrumental, apparent). What are the bases of inferential confidence you are employing? For example, what do citations measure, and can we legitimately count and compare such data? How reliable is the peer review/refereeing process? What precisely does the concept of relevance denote in the context of information retrieval?

Management

How is the research to be conducted: in-house and on a do-it-yourself basis, by hiring consultants, on a multiclient basis? On an agreed customer-contractor basis? Is the study premium quality or quick-and-dirty in character? Who "owns" the results?

Kind of Research

How should the research be characterized: basic, pure, strategic, applied, problem solving, developmental?

Time Horizon

What time frame is envisaged: short-term versus long-term; a one-off snapshot versus time lapsed; rolling versus longitudinal data gathering?

Even a nonexhaustive classification such as this can be beneficial. It helps you map out the range of research options in terms of inputs, processes, and outputs, and thus achieve a better fit between problem and investigative strategy.

PICKING PROBLEMS

Defining a research problem as anything that rouses curiosity, or as any activity for which research funds are forthcoming, is perhaps a trifle disingenuous. In effect, the flood gates are open, and almost any kind of puzzle or difficulty achieves research status. This may not matter greatly, though purists and the priesthood may sometimes bridle at what passes for research.

Why should librarians be interested in research? Such a question invites a potential litany of Motherhood and Apple Pie statements, but it can also be answered by the word "survival." To quote Swisher and McClure (1984):

> The myriad constraints which librarians must confront in the foreseeable future will demand greater accountability for decision making. . . . Research

that directly supports decision making is not an altruistic pursuit, only for those who have the time and the interest; it is a survival skill, essential for the continued vitality of library/information services. (p. xiii)

Line (1991), however, is less apocalyptic, preferring to speak in terms of a general research-mindedness or disposition, which, of course, results in the admission of virtually any kind of inquiry or investigation no matter how local, focused, trivial, or small-scale:

Practitioners need to look critically at all activities, past, present and possible future, and approach their work in a constantly experimental and enquiring frame of mind: what would happen if I tried so-and-so, how best can I do so-and-so, and how can I find out how well we are doing so-and-so and how well it worked? Research-mindedness should be an automatic mode of thought, a way of life. Not all of this will result in research, and much of it will be of purely local interest, but some will be of much wider interest. (p. 6)

With the justification firmly in place, the next step is to identify candidate problems that can be researched. Numerous checklists and guidelines can be found in the general survey research literature and in the literature of librarianship. Typical guiding criteria for applied or action research will include:

Actionability

Is change (as suggested by the research) within the control of the library, and can appropriate recommendations be implemented as desired? If we can't do something with what we've done, why do it?

Definition

Can the problem be clearly formulated and its essence conveyed to others?

Congruence

Does the problem under investigation relate strongly to the mission and objectives of the library or to those of the parent institution?

Centrality

Does the problem domain/focus account for a significant consumption of resources (human, material, financial, or technical) or is it of marginal concern?

Externality

Does the problem under investigation impact significantly on the activities, needs, or perceptions of users?

Utility

Is it reasonable to assume that the results of the research effort will have value-in-use?

Communicability

Can the import of the research results be transmitted clearly and effectively to the target audience in such a way as to ensure effective adoption?

AVOIDING PITFALLS

Assuming satisfactory answers are forthcoming for each of the above, the next step is to anticipate as many as possible of the pitfalls that await the unsuspecting researcher. If common sense is not enough, there are textbooks aplenty with solid advice on what to do and what not to do. The list of caveats and problems that follows is an adaptation of Swisher and McClure (1984):

Problem Statement

- Lacks focus . . . too diffuse
- Poorly expressed
- Low organizational relevance/salience
- Assumptions underlying the problem are ignored

Prior Art

- Failure to conduct cross-field literature searches (n.b., Swanson's [1990] concept of logically related but noninterconnecting literature sets)
- Unintentional duplication of research
- Ignores grey literature (e.g., in-house/unpublished studies)
- Not invented here (NIH) syndrome

Definitions

- Unanchored terminology
- Lack of consistency or precision in data categorization or analysis
- Terms may be defined but not operationalized (i.e., cannot be measured)
- Definitions at variance with existing standards (i.e., idiomatic usage)

Methodology

- No formal or agreed research plan/agenda
- Investigative methods/tools inappropriate to problem
- Failure to identify hidden costs
- Deficient know-how/technical expertise

Findings/Results

- Limitations of results are not stated explicitly (e.g., sampling error, confidence levels, experimenter bias, reliability)
- Significance or implications of findings not clearly perceived or stated
- Inability to translate results into actionable recommendations (e.g., politically unacceptable, nontransferrable across cultures)

Utility

- Presentation of results lacks clarity
- Results do not lead to improved organizational effectiveness
- Results evoke "So what?" response

SOFT FACTORS . . . SOFT CITATION

The kind of literature alluded to in this paper makes little or no reference to the role of intuition in either the conception or prosecution of research. Words like "aha," "eureka," "insight," "hunch," "epiphany," are noticeable by their absence. This is unfortunate. What we say elsewhere with respect to information management practice applies equally to the research process:

> You cannot teach people intuition, but you can help them trust their own judgment by making them aware of how it has been formed, and of the biases and prejudices which are brought into play. . . . We believe that intuition is as valuable to management as scientism. The soft models we invoke (from metaphor to matrix) can be used to foster intuition. (Cronin & Davenport, 1991, p. 185)

Metaphor, for example, encourages people to see things in a different light, to seek out echoes and parallels, and to think laterally. It is a valuable modeling tool that can be put to good use in the formulation and conduct of research. The researcher who is a whiz at discriminant function analysis and linear programming may still lack the necessary sensitivity and flexibility to spot really interesting research issues or to interpret the full significance of his/her results. Research, in other words, is not a mechanistic activity (beware what Ortega y Gasset [1960] calls the "terrorism of the laboratories"). Ideally, it combines an enquiring mind with investigative literacy. But let me illustrate what I mean about metaphor with a personal example.

One of my current research interests is exploring the social and cognitive significance of acknowledgments in the scholarly communication process (Cronin, 1991). Until now, the role and status of acknowledgments have been virtually ignored in the literature of our own field: Our attention has focused instead on citations and how they can be used to measure research performance and communication patterns among scientists and researchers. I have been carrying out citation studies intermittently for a decade, but I had never thought of the acknowledgment as a logical extension of my interest in citation analysis. I was not looking for a fresh research topic, nor was I trying to build upon my previous bibliometric work when it dawned on me that there was a degree of functional equivalence between citation and acknowledgment. When we cite another's work we are, to a greater or lesser extent, acknowledging the influence of that individual's thinking on our own cogitations. When we include a personal acknowledgment at the end of a published paper, we are making a public statement of gratitude for services rendered, which may be technical assistance, intellectual stimulation, or whatever.

Acknowledgments often function as "soft citations," metaphorically speaking. The mere act of reconceptualizing acknowledgment as soft citation has dragged acknowledgment practice out of the penumbra and opened up a potentially rich research vein for myself and others. But, to return to the title of this talk, at no time did I view acknowledgment as problematic; at no time did I reflect on the problem status of research into the communication role of acknowledgments. Now, however, I can see that there may be a logical (even moral) problem in excluding acknowledgments, but not citations, from individual and institutional evaluation exercises, and that further research is called for if this apparent anomaly is to be resolved.

What qualities, then, are needed to be a good researcher? Apart from the obvious (e.g., proficiency in research techniques), I would cite three from my own experience: curiosity, passion, and deep knowledge of one's field. But that is a highly personal view, one that reflects the fact that the longer I remain in this field and the more I learn, the greater the number of research topics that suggest themselves. But I shall leave it to my mentor and former colleague, John Martyn (Moore, 1987), to define the attributes that go to make up a good (funded) researcher:

> What makes a good researcher is firstly a total determination to keep to the deadlines in the project, secondly a decent respect for the tax payers' money that he or she lives on, thirdly a desire to do something genuinely useful as opposed to merely interesting, fourthly a combination of objectivity,

a legalistic view of what constitutes evidence, a mind open to different interpretations of what the evidence may mean and a lot of imagination, fifthly a degree of numeracy, sixthly the ability to write up the results clearly, concisely and preferably amusingly, and seventhly a well-developed awareness that most people, especially researchers, have got it wrong most of the time. (p. vii-viii)

ACKNOWLEDGMENTS

I am grateful to Colin Harris, Steve Harter, and Judith Serebnick for constructive comments on earlier drafts of this paper.

REFERENCES

Bookstein, A. (1990a). Informetric distributions, part I: Unified overview. *Journal of the American Society for Information Science, 41*(5), 368-375.

Bookstein, A. (1990b). Informetric distributions, part II: Resilience to ambiguity. *Journal of the American Society for Information Science, 41*(5), 376-386.

Close, F. (1990). *Too hot to handle: The race for cold fusion.* London: W. H. Allen.

Cronin, B. (1980). *Direct mail advertising and public library use.* London: British Library (British Library Research & Development Report No. 5539).

Cronin, B. (1991). Let the credits roll: A preliminary examination of the role played by mentors and trusted assessors in disciplinary formation. *Journal of Documentation, 47*(3), 227-239.

Cronin, B., & Davenport, E. (1990). Laptops and the marketing information chain: The benefits of salesforce automation. *International Journal of Information Management, 10*(4), 278-287.

Cronin, B., & Davenport, E. (1991). *Elements of information management.* Metuchen, NJ: Scarecrow Press.

Gieryn, T. F. (1978). Problem retention and problem change in science. In J. Gaston (Ed.), *Sociology of science* (pp. 96-115). San Francisco, CA: Jossey-Bass.

Line, M. B. (1991). Research policy in librarianship and information science: Keynote address. In C. Harris (Ed.), *Research policy in librarianship and information science* (pp. 1-10). London: Taylor Graham.

Moore, N. (1987). *How to do research* (2nd ed). London: Library Association.

Ortega y Gasset, J. (1960). *What is philosophy?* New York: W. W. Norton.

Overholser, C. (1986). Quality, quantity, and thinking real hard. *Journal of Advertising Research, 26*(3), RC-7—RC-12.

Patton, M. Q. (1986). *Utilization-focused evaluation* (2nd ed.). Newbury Park, CA: Sage Publications.

Russell, B. (1959). *The problems of philosophy.* New York: Oxford University Press.

Swanson, D. R. (1990). The absence of co-citation as a clue to undiscovered causal connections. In C. L. Borgman (Ed.), *Scholarly communication and bibliometrics* (pp. 129-137). Newbury Park, CA: Sage Publications.

Swisher, R., & McClure, C. R. (1984). *Research for decision making: Methods for librarians.* Chicago: American Library Association.

Zweizig, D. L. (1973). *Predicting amount of library use: An empirical study of the role of the public library in the life of the adult public.* Doctoral dissertation, Syracuse University, Syracuse, NY.

DEBRA WILCOX JOHNSON

Assistant Professor
School of Library and Information Studies
University of Wisconsin-Madison

Roles in the Research Process

ABSTRACT

Two groups—practitioners and faculty/researchers—top the list of key players in the research process, which also includes state and federal library agencies, associations, consultants, the business sector, and users. Key functions of these groups include generating ideas, numbers gathering, and producing research. Also important to the research process are the consumer or user of research, participation in research studies, funding, and dissemination of research results.

INTRODUCTION

The topic of roles in the research process requires first that two concepts be defined: research and roles. For the purpose of this paper, the term research is defined very broadly to encompass basic, applied, and action research including needs assessment and evaluation. This perspective is used in order to be as inclusive as possible for both researchers and practitioners. Although this would not be a universally accepted definition, this approach incorporates the idea of a continuum, with one end being the gathering of information for immediate decision making and the other end being the "big questions" or basic research.

The concept of roles, in this context, can be interpreted in two ways. First, people can look at roles as functions, which raises the question, "What are the functions necessary to the research process?" Second, one can examine the individuals, groups, or institutions that play a role in the research process. By combining these two interpretations, the question addressed in this essay is, "Who are the players in the research process and how do they relate to the research roles or functions?"

THE RESEARCH PLAYERS

At the simplest level, it is easy to say that everyone has a role to play in the research process. This very general grouping, however, has been defined by speakers during the Allerton conference as containing two key groups: practitioners and faculty/researchers. The practitioner has been referred to in various ways, most often as library administrator, although the label "user-savvy" practitioner provides another insightful description. The other primary players are library and information science educators and researchers. In terms of productivity, when defined as publication, these two groups are the source for much of the study in library and information science.

Within these broad categories, however, other groups participate in the research process. State library agencies, the U.S. Department of Education Library Programs, and associations (state, regional, and national) certainly have a role to play in research. The list also would not be complete without adding consultants, who are often drawn from the practitioner and educator pools. Increasingly, the research work in the field is being done by consultants, although the work may not become part of the regular publication stream. Added to the list of players are an increasing number of research firms not necessarily based in the library and information science field. Although this is not necessarily a negative occurrence, it may have an effect on dissemination of research results since these researchers tend to work in different disciplines and publish outside the library literature.

The business sector is another group that participates in the research process. This work can be less visible to the field. It is the research and development (R&D) function of the companies, and the results are reflected in the products that companies develop. What is not clear is the effect or influence of research within the field on product development. For example, does the extensive body of work on use of the catalog influence the research on and the development of commercially available online catalogs?

A subset of the business sector includes publishing. In the dissemination of research results, publishers, editors, and editorial boards play a critical role.

Finally, when talking about participants in the research process, users (and nonusers) logically complete the list. Not all research can be unobtrusive, and relying solely on the "traces" of use or the observation technique has limits. To explain, for example, the "whys" of use or nonuse, willing participants are necessary.

What groups, then, have a potential role in the research process? Two groups—practitioners and faculty/researchers—top the list, which also includes state and federal library agencies, associations, consultants, the business sector, and users. If one examines the amount of research that is published or is conducted, the groups just described would be responsible for the majority of that work in a variety of settings.

FUNCTIONS IN THE RESEARCH PROCESS

Using as examples some of the players identified in the first section, what are some of the key functions that are evident in the research process? In this paper, several will be identified, including three major roles: generating ideas, numbers gathering, and producing research. Although discussed individually, these roles or functions are not mutually exclusive; a debate over which activity fits within which function seems unimportant here. It is more important to understand that in addition to crossover in the roles, one function is necessary for another to occur. Likewise, the roles coexist. All the roles need to be in place for an effective research community.

Generating Ideas

The first function in the research process is to generate ideas. This process can be the most creative, energizing, and entertaining part of the research effort. It sounds simplistic, but idea generation is a crucial step toward answering the "right questions." What are the issues to be considered, and what are the new ways to ask the questions? In the workplace, this idea generation is reflected in questions such as, "Why does this happen?" or "What if we do this?" Faculty are bemused when a doctoral student says, "I can really only think of one thing to do for a dissertation." The response is, "Read and think more, then come back!"

There is no limit on the number of questions that can be examined within information agencies and by researchers. Given this fact, priorities are being set—personally, within institutions, and by the field. One manifestation of this priority setting is a "research agenda." Currently a national research agenda exists, developed under the auspices of the U.S. Department of Education. Another example is the Association of College and Research Libraries (ACRL) research agenda. Credit for that product is given to three steps: thinking about ideas, articulating key questions, and setting priorities for researchers.

When considering the various players within this function, one can consider two aspects: the field (or practice) and the discipline of library and information studies. The practice of the discipline or the profession supplies ideas to the research process, as reflected in activities such as publishing, conference programming, and funding priorities. Likewise, the discipline of library and information studies is reflected in the profession. Sharing ideas is crucial to both. A necessary role for the practitioner is to articulate and prioritize the needs of the profession.

Library and information science educators also have a role to play in generating research ideas. Some of the questions will be in response to their professional activities, but others are a result of "knowing the literature." It is a reasonable expectation that library faculty are responsible for keeping abreast of what is going on in the field, i.e., to see the broad spectrum. Separated from a particular type of information agency, faculty can look at the context for issues in practice and bring to the profession literature from outside the field. Researchers draw from psychology, public administration, adult education, sociology, and communication, to name a few. This broader perspective contributes to generating research ideas.

For faculty who carry out this function, a picture comes to mind from the movie *The Wizard of Oz*. When the Scarecrow gets his diploma, it is a "doctor of thinkology" degree. Faculty need more time to be doctors of thinkology, generating and discussing research ideas. More opportunities, such as the University of Illinois summer research retreat, are important for concentrating on the process of idea generation.

In addition to practitioners and faculty, other agencies play a role in this process. Certainly the U.S. Department of Education assumes an important role in sponsoring a national research agenda for the discipline and in setting priorities for federal research funding. Another player is the state library agency. One of its key roles is to identify, within a state, trends, issues, opportunities, and needs. Certainly none of the players noted in the previous section is exempt from the idea-generation experience.

Numbers Gathering

A second role in the research process is difficult to name precisely, but it is sometimes referred to as "numbers gathering" or "number crunching." Some research methodologies and designs require collecting and analyzing numbers, but the function referred to in this section is the work being done to collect numbers without really having a specific research question in mind. Probably one of the most extensive examples is the effort of approximately 8,000 U.S. public libraries to annually contribute data to a federal database, the Federal-State Cooperative System (FSCS). Similar types of data collection exist for other types of information agencies.

The issue with this regular "numbers gathering" is that the results can be used in the research process. Other speakers at the Allerton conference have urged listeners to make use of existing data sources. When used in the research continuum described earlier, the numbers help make day-to-day decisions while also being a source for basic research. Researchers analyze these numbers in new ways and in different combinations.

These kind of data aid in identifying anomalies or gaps that lead to further research. For example, why is library circulation lower for senior citizens than for the rest of the adult population? These numbers also document problems, such as underutilized resources or decreasing financial support. The numbers-gathering role is an important part of the research process, since it leads to asking new questions, while answering others. Existing data sources are extensive and can be tapped for projects along the research continuum.

What players carry out the numbers-gathering role? In the case of public libraries, state library agencies coordinate the annual data collection, as well as collect data from other types of libraries and on numerous topics. Local libraries regularly collect counts of library circulation, reference transactions, and interlibrary loan traffic, along with collection and budget figures. The commitment of the local library to produce accurate and timely information is basic to the success of these numbers-gathering efforts.

In evaluating library services, the source of information is at the local level. For example, as library involvement in adult literacy is studied, a vital question is, "How does the individual change as a result of participation in the library's adult literacy program?" Since it is the staff of the local literacy program who are close to learners, the staff are the ones to assess changes. This information, in the aggregate, is then passed up through the system—a bottom-up rather than a top-down model of data gathering. Information comes from local agencies, it is consolidated, and results are brought forward so that they are useful for a broader group of people.

Professional associations can take on the numbers-gathering function. An example of this is the Public Library Data Service, produced for the Public Library Association by the University of Wisconsin-Madison. Other examples are the salary surveys conducted by the American Library Association under the guidance of Mary Jo Lynch.

Is there enough numbers gathering going on? It depends on a person's perspective. The local librarian may complain that too much is being asked for, whereas the historian feels that too little of the library's efforts are being documented for future study. Although one might bemoan the extent of numbers gathering currently going on, it may be better to lament the lack of use of such rich sources of information.

Producing Research

A third function in the research process is, most logically, to produce research—creating the research product. The definition of that function is fairly straightforward: a commitment to research and then carrying out the work. But the question of who is producing research is more complex. When people attempt to split practitioners and faculty into two "camps," this becomes dysfunctional for the field and the discipline. Basic research, applied research, and action research occur in both groups. When it comes to producing research, however, faculty efforts may have different purposes.

For educators, the role of producing research is manifested in four ways in the library and information science discipline. First, there is the faculty member's personal research agenda. This may distinguish this group from practitioners, since library staff are usually bound by the needs of the institution when conducting research. In contrast, faculty members designate their research interests, known as a "research stream." Undoubtedly, the availability of funding affects that research focus, but in reality faculty have a great deal of flexibility in determining their research agendas.

A second way in which library schools contribute to research production is through Ph.D. programs. An increasing number of students are completing Ph.D. degrees. Much of the discipline's basic research rests in Ph.D. dissertations (which, unfortunately, are not widely used).

Faculty also produce research via consulting. This aspect of faculty productivity is usually referred to as "service" in higher education. In this capacity, faculty, working within a specific institution or set of institutions, conduct applied and action research.

Finally, library schools produce research via formal research centers. The Library Research Center at the University of Illinois is the oldest in existence, maintaining its effort for over 30 years. Clarion's (Pennsylvania) center focuses on rural librarianship, whereas the University of Wisconsin-Madison's center for Library Evaluation and Development (LEAD) builds on its strengths in evaluation. These centers not only try to attract research work to the schools, but also can coordinate research being done by the faculty. The centers also become a training ground for both practitioners and Ph.D. students through employment on research projects. The centers are a fourth way in which library education is responding to the need for research.

Libraries, and therefore the staff, also are research producers. This effort is not completely documented, except anecdotally, although some of the work results in publication. Given that library-based research has as one of its goals to aid in decision making, it is likely to be categorized as applied or action research. Evaluation and needs assessment studies typify these efforts and result in a large number of studies. For example, St. Louis Public Library at this conference reported completing over 50 such studies. If cooperative and multitype systems research efforts are added, it becomes evident that even within the public library community, the amount of research work being done is much larger than what is found in regular library publications.

Increased rigor in practitioner research is a continuing need. Another concern is that the local studies have limited dissemination. Naturally, the library studies tend to be "institutionally bound," focusing on unique characteristics of the setting. One of the challenges facing librarians who produce research is to place that research into a broader context, building on previous work in the area. Writers who extrapolate features applicable in a number of libraries will make the research product more useful when shared at conferences and prepared for publication. This helps avoid the exclusively "how we did good" articles.

State libraries have an opportunity to produce research through commissioned studies and "fast response" research. This approach is typified by the Colorado State Library through the work of Keith Lance. A useful image for this kind of research comes from Ron Dubberly, the director of the Atlanta-Fulton County Public Library. He refers to "ninja evaluation." The process is to zero in on a very specific question, get useful information quickly, process the information gathered, and then use the results. Colorado State Library conducts, among other things, "ninja research" as effectively reported in their "Fast Facts" publication. State libraries have the resources and the network to gather information in a timely fashion to respond to the needs of the state's library community. State library agencies also produce a number of regular reports, noted in the previous section, as well as special research reports conducted in-house or by contract.

When examining research productivity, associations contribute at all levels of the organization, including committees. For example, the Medical Library Association, via its research committee, conducted a continuing education needs assessment of its membership. The American Library Association also recently produced a children's output measures manual.

A final example of this role is the case of the private consultant or consulting firm. On behalf of libraries, associations, and so on, the consultant produces research reports on a broad range of topics, from automation to library cooperation. The reports generally are produced in small numbers and, as a result, have limited distribution. Although the studies are sometimes announced to the library community, only a few are shared via the library press.

Given the use of a continuum to define research in this paper, it is not surprising that many players contribute to the role of producing research. Each group has constraints that affect the nature and availability of the research being produced.

Consumer of Research Results

This essay concentrates on three principal roles in the research process: idea generation, numbers gathering, and producing research. Others can be added to the list, although they require less explanation. One of these is the role of consumer or user of research. Using research for decision making, clarifying, explaining, and justifying strengthens the ties between the theory and practice of library and information studies. The consumer or user functions as the feedback loop in the research process. As results are critically reviewed and used, the ensuing insights lead to revised questions, improved methods, and added areas for investigation.

Unfortunately, anecdotal evidence combined with citation studies show that a great deal of research is never used, let alone read. Given that the profession is based on information seeking and reading, this is a disturbing observation. As more graduate schools incorporate research methods in the curriculum and make more use of research in teaching, new professionals may become better consumers of research. When designing research projects, faculty as well as practitioners can draw from previous work. A lack of awareness leads to "reinventing the wheel." For example, from numerous catalog use studies, it is repeatedly found that education level affects catalog use. Given the consistency of that finding, is this a necessary feature for every study of catalog use? Another example can be drawn from library needs assessment. It is of no surprise that books for circulation ranks consistently among the top services offered by public libraries, yet this continues to be included in user surveys.

During a recent seminar, one participant recommended that library administrators require all memos to be documented with citations from the literature, especially research findings. One could ask, "Why should a literature-based field need this requirement?" Yet, this policy potentially could serve a useful function. Requiring references to the literature to support assumptions and clarify issues could generate more use of the research being produced in the field, including internal documents, reports, and statistics. Consultants working with libraries to conduct community studies will find that the library has already collected extensive data. The need often is not for further data but to make sense of what is already available.

Ultimately for the discipline of library and information studies, the desire is for consumers to include people from other fields and disciplines. This truly completes the cyclical research process. This means that the work in this field not only draws on other disciplines, but contributes new perspectives and findings to those other fields.

Participation in Research Studies

Another function, and for researchers a very important function, is participation in research studies. Although identifying participation as a role in the research process may be stating the obvious, the success of several research designs is dependent upon that cooperation. The concept of "return rate" or "participation rate" permeates the research process.

The federal government recognizes the value of this role. On contracts that require gathering data from subjects, investigators are asked to calculate the "response burden." Basically, this is an estimate of the amount of time needed from each participant, multiplied by the number of people involved. This gives the burden (in terms of time) for the targeted population. Groups with high response burdens are less likely to agree to participate. As more library-based research is conducted, practitioners and users potentially will respond negatively to their response burdens. This makes agreement to participate a serious role in the research process.

Related to the role of participation is the idea of the library as laboratory. In this case, the institution is studied or becomes a testing ground for new services and techniques. Throughout the Allerton conference, references have been made to host libraries, test sites, and case studies, all of which relate to the library as laboratory. For example, at the University of Wisconsin-Madison, two recent studies involved the public library as laboratory—the Urban Library Council's financial practices study and a family literacy project. These types of studies are possible only because of full institutional cooperation.

Involvement in the research process is not a one-way street for information agencies. Often, insights into their own practices derive from contact with researchers, and research reports can serve as a focal point for staff review and discussion.

Funding

Although the phrase "money makes the world go round" may be too cynical, it is clear that funding is necessary for the work of research. Even when costs are incorporated into a library's regular budget, the resources need to be there in the first place. Release time for research, especially for tenure-track academic librarians, is another type of support needed to enhance research productivity. To conduct multi-institutional studies or experiments requires more than local budgets can provide and usually requires outside grants and contracts.

Although the concept of funding as a role in the research process requires little definition, funding (current and potential) comes from a wide range of sources. Libraries provide research dollars for single-institution studies. These projects may require the use of consultants. Also, the library's ability to garner grants for new services and projects allows an opportunity to fund evaluation research as a component of these efforts. Grant proposal budgets can include dollars for evaluation of the project. Libraries may be the only eligible applicants for some grant programs. By incorporating a research-based evaluation component, libraries become a source of funding for evaluation research.

Historically, the U.S. Department of Education has been a source for basic library research and development funding. In the past ten years, this funding allowed for about three to five projects annually. The dollars have always been limited; during the 1992 funding cycle, no funds were available for field-initiated research projects. Other federal sources outside Library Programs have funded research, especially in the information science arena.

Other examples of funding include OCLC grants for basic research, and the Council on Library Resources (CLR) is a source for major studies as well as for practitioner/faculty collaborative projects. The collaborative CLR grants provide seed money for institution-based studies.

Associations have also increased their support for research. For example, the American Library Association annually gives the Baber Research Award, the Special Libraries Association provides a research award, and the Association for Library and Information Science Education awards a grant for research related to education in the discipline.

Although a wide range of sources may be available, the process is competitive. Private sources via foundations continue to be important for the research process. Ongoing, consistent funding levels from all sources are essential to carrying the field and discipline forward.

Dissemination

Dissemination of research is the companion role to that of consumer of research. Before research can be used, it must be available in a timely fashion and in a form that is usable by a broad range of consumers. The analogy may be that of the tree that falls but no one hears it. If research is done but not disseminated, is it research, is it useful, and is it part of the process? Given the number of players in the research effort, the amount of work that is published in the field's journals or in monograph form represents just a percentage of the total effort. This situation is compounded when potential consumers of the research have access to only a limited number of journals or have a preference for professional publications over primarily research journals.

The ability to report research results in professional journals is countered by the requirements for faculty tenure and promotion. Writing for research and refereed journals is valued more highly in higher education than those articles in professional publications.

To aid in dissemination, information agencies can identify a person in the organization who is willing to serve as research "gatekeeper." As studies are identified and reviewed by the gatekeeper, pertinent items can be summarized for staff or routed for further study. This model is not unknown to the field, as it parallels specialized programs offered to patrons such as current awareness services or selective dissemination of information. Some published sources can assist in this effort, such as the *Public Library Watch,* published by the University of Illinois Library Research Center, and research notes in some journals. A complement to this effort is to assign staff attending conferences to cover rescarch programs.

Another facet of dissemination is the publication of evaluation results from local projects. As noted earlier in this essay, too little of the internal research effort is shared outside the institution. This is also reflected in the limited availability of consultants' reports. When seeking outside funds to support studies, libraries can consider requesting enough funding to allow for multiple copies of the final report. This helps meet the demand for research reports announced in the library press or mentioned at conference programs.

Library educators have an additional contribution to make to the dissemination role besides their publication efforts. Research publications and results incorporated in reading lists and classroom work introduce the research in the field to students. Integrating use of research in the education of new professionals may increase the likelihood that this will occur in the workplace. Modeling use of research for students encourages emulation of that behavior throughout their careers.

Continuing education institutes and workshops provide another opportunity to incorporate research into teaching and to apply it to practice. This translates into talking about research in such a way that people can see its usefulness in their own situation.

Associations contribute to the dissemination role through conference offerings and publications. Greater attention can be given to including articles that synthesize a body of research in association publications. This can serve as a useful starting place for interested readers.

Other Roles

Beyond those introduced in this essay, additional roles can be named. Among these is an advocacy for research role, that is, encouraging, recognizing, and rewarding effective research. On the other side, the research process needs someone to carry on the role of skeptic, challenging assumptions used and helping to ensure rigor in the research process.

Others take on the role of advisor to research projects, typically through membership on advisory or expert panels. This has the benefit of blending the expertise of researchers, practitioners, users, and others.

Training and educating current and future researchers is a role necessary to increase research productivity and to improve the quality of research. If the field is expected to conduct research, the skills need to be present. As noted earlier, graduate schools offer (and some require) research methods courses. Continuing education workshops in the research process and techniques also are used to prepare researchers or enhance skills.

CONCLUSION

This essay attempts to define the research process in terms of the functions or roles that exist in order for research to flourish. In addition, different players contribute to each of these roles.

The perspective presented here is a collaborative one. Both the practice and the discipline of library and information science have a place in this collaborative model of the research process. To talk about them and us, researchers versus practitioners, pure versus applied research, or big questions and little problems is detrimental to moving the field and discipline forward. Besides avoiding these dichotomies, each participant in the research process needs to recognize the value of contributions made along the research continuum described at the start of this essay.

The variety of research approaches used, the diversity of questions and problems posed, and the number of players create a rich source of current and future research. In the final analysis, however, perhaps one more feature should be added to the research process: striving for excellence in research. This corresponds to excellence in practice and, ultimately, to making a difference in the lives of the people being served by information agencies.

DWIGHT F. BURLINGAME

Director for Academic Programs and Research
Center on Philanthropy
Indiana University
Indianapolis, Indiana

Getting Your Money's Worth: Negotiating with Research Agencies

ABSTRACT

When seeking grants from a funding agency, the grantwriter must first engage in some pre-proposal research. This stage includes communicating with the agency to make sure a project fits the funder's mission and that it meets eligibility requirements and other guidelines. A telephone contact or face-to-face contact may be appropriate. When writing the formal proposal, the grantwriter should indicate budget, methods of evaluation and dissemination, and follow other recommended techniques for effective proposal writing. After the proposal is written, it will be reviewed by the funding agency staff, and the grantwriter will have to answer any questions raised by the agency.

INTRODUCTION

One of the potentially most difficult tasks that any grantwriter faces is negotiating with potential funders. After all, they have the money, and you want some of it. Upon initial examination, this appears to be a power situation in which the grantseeker is at a definite disadvantage. However, upon further reflection, perhaps it is not so.

PRE-PROPOSAL RESEARCH

Before negotiation can begin, two parties have to want to accomplish a particular goal. On the part of the grantseeker, it is imperative to have articulated a project that clearly defines what is to be accomplished that fits the grantmaker's mission. Certainly you already know this because you have done your library research (after all—who is better qualified than a librarian to have made absolutely sure what previous grants have been made, to whom, and for what amounts).

Communication with the foundation, granting agency, or donor to ascertain sponsor interest begins the negotiation process. A clear understanding of eligibility requirements, proposal guidelines, deadlines for submission and review cycles, what can be funded (e.g., overhead, capital costs, books), funding levels and usual level of competition, and what similar projects have been funded (with insights gained by discussion with previous recipients and a thorough reading of annual reports) will ultimately assist the grantseeker in leveling the playing field upon which negotiation will take place. A telephone contact with the potential funder is appropriate to ascertain that your proposed project fits within the funder's guidelines—for sure.

If appropriate, you should inquire about visiting with the potential grantor or donor regarding your proposed research. Face-to-face contact provides another opportunity to minimize the power differential and thus facilitate the negotiation process. Building a relationship is crucial to long-term success. How you build rapport will often depend upon the type of foundation (large or small, corporate or private, family member living or dead, national or local in scope) or granting agency. There is no single foundation cultural. Being in the same community facilitates collaboration and partnerships. Too many proposals attempt to stretch the potential donor or grantmaker beyond their area of interest. The reverse can also be true. That is, the proposal writer, often under perceived pressure to get a grant in order to gain tenure, salary enhancement, or recognition, develops a proposal that does not fit the mission of the institution. Community foundations are a rapidly growing segment that library researchers should be reviewing.

If your telephone call and visit has indicated an interest in your work, a written pre-proposal to the funding agency is the best way to confirm interest and to open the dialogue that will lead to the major proposal. A short and concise two to three pages that clearly state what the grantor is being requested to fund, the significance of the research, who will be involved (Are there other researchers working on this issue? Are you collaborating?), why the issue needs to be researched, and how your research is supported by your home institution is all that is needed. A perceived fit between your request and the foundation's or donor's interest is a must to begin a negotiation.

THE FORMAL PROPOSAL

The formal proposal will ultimately be the document from which you and the grantmaker negotiate. Therefore, it is incumbent for you to indicate how much you are requesting illustrated in a reasonably detailed budget, how it is to be accomplished, and how the work will be evaluated and disseminated. Discussion of how you plan to disseminate your results is especially important because it is one of the major ways by which the funder evaluates if its resources will benefit the public good. The format for your formal proposal will, of course, vary depending upon the funder's guidelines and expectations. However, be sure to focus your project (do not try to solve the world's problems). But do not become parochial and certainly avoid what is commonly known in the grantmaker world as "continuing doctorate syndrome." What is it that you are doing that relates to the "public good?"

Among all the proposal tips or tricks offered by experts and from personal experience, I would emphasize techniques that guide the reader to what they seek. In other words, use a table of contents, key headings, and key phrases that address the issues that the funder has articulated. Use concise language with attention-getting statements. In other words, KISS—Keep It Short and Simple. Even though it is trite, it bears repeating since in our last review of proposals, at least half failed to do this very thing. It may be that so much of proposal writing and fund-raising falls under the rubric of "of course" information. That is, we skip over what we think we know and don't learn from it. Countless funders have been heard to echo the refrain—"They didn't learn what they already know." (See Gooch [1987], Grant & Berkowitz [1988], and Priest & Clark [1990] for other suggestions.)

REVIEW STAGE

Staff review of your proposal will often produce a set of questions and concerns for you to answer. This is really the point at which you get to test your negotiation skills. A careful review of the questions raised by the agency or donor mandates a response to those that you can address and an explanation of why you cannot meet certain other requests. Do not be timid in explaining why you prefer a certain approach or why "x" cannot be accomplished in this proposal. Forthright and honest responses will enhance your position. It is imperative to remember as you attempt to balance the power differential that the funder cannot carry out the project. They need you to do this. Without you and others like you, one part of the philanthropic equation would be lost, and thus no action could take place and the entire process would cease to exist. Remember, however, if you are negotiating with a foundation program officer, they must also sell your proposal to their board before it can get funded. It behooves the grantmaker to work with you in building the strongest case for your proposal.

As in most negotiation, knowing why you may not win is important information to build your strategy upon, so is the case in grantseeking. The following eight reasons why your proposal may not succeed are offered as a review check:

1. The need has not been demonstrated.
2. The proposal does not fit the potential funder's goals.
3. It is poorly written.
4. The budget is not in the range of the funding source.
5. The project is too ambitious.
6. The guidelines for submission were not followed.
7. It does not appear that the grantseeker has the capabilities to carry out the project.
8. The methods and/or evaluation are not clear, or they are inadequate.

Finally, let me encourage you to keep trying. The fund-raising cycle is a constant one of developing relationships based upon a shared mission, asking, giving, and recognition. Such a process cannot take place without two parties at the negotiation table. Both are crucial.

REFERENCES

Gooch, J. M. (1987). *Writing winning proposals.* Washington, DC: Council for Advancement and Support of Education.

Grant, A., & Berkowitz, E. S. (1988). Knowledge is power: Learn about prospects before you write your proposals. *Currents, 14*(9), 6-9.

Priest, S., & Clark, D. (1990). Help yourself: Guide to getting grants. *Journal of Experiential Education, 13*(1), 31-37.

GAIL D. McCLURE

Director of Communication
W. K. Kellogg Foundation
Battle Creek, Michigan

The W. K. Kellogg Foundation and Human Resource Development in Information Science

ABSTRACT

Human resource development in information science is an "emerging program priority area" for the W. K. Kellogg Foundation, and hence a potential area for funding by the Foundation. By understanding how foundations like the W. K. Kellogg Foundation work—their philosophy, their structure, their rules and regulations, their founding, their governing boards, and their past and current projects—a potential grantee can determine if a particular foundation is an appropriate funding source for his or her area of interest.

INFORMATION SCIENCE AS AN EMERGING PROGRAM PRIORITY AREA

The W. K. Kellogg Foundation is interested in libraries for several reasons. At the Foundation, we have what we call an emerging program priority area called Human Resource Development for Management of Information Systems. When we label something as an emerging program priority, we believe the area has some significant social value, and we want to study it and begin to formulate a program around it. For example, the most recent emerging program priority area was family and neighborhoods. Over the past two years, we moved slowly to build our understanding of where we could make a unique contribution to families and neighborhoods, and we are just now beginning to make grants against that framework.

When people see the phrase "emerging program priority area" in our annual report, they often ask, "What does that mean?" It means we are in an exploration process, and we explore in several ways. We do it by sending people like me to meetings like the Allerton conference, where we listen to what is being said and try to get a sense of what the issues are. We do it by having information science questions embedded in our reviews of related proposals and by asking knowledgeable grantees and fellows what they think critical issues are related to the priority. We also do it by reading and sharing information with other foundations and donors. In general, we try to get an idea of professional, academic, and user perspectives. Then we gradually put a picture together of the issues in the area, and we analyze those issues against our philosophy, goals, and strategies to formulate a plan that will help direct our grantmaking.

The reason that our board decided we should focus our interest on the human resource aspects of information science as an emerging priority area is our focus on social change. We are interested in information science as it can help effect that change. We believe that a fundamental change in information management is needed to better understand the new world of information, especially as it relates to teaching and learning. And while hardware and software technologies are developing quickly, there seems to be a limitation on the development of human resources to manage these new systems and to assist others in accessing and using information in a meaningful way.

Let me give you an idea of how we approach developing an emerging program priority area. We spend a lot of time looking at the institutions and professions that were critical during the development of the country. We find that many of them are struggling at present. Formed in the 19th century and the early part of this century, they are beginning to lose their identity and are struggling to remain relevant to today's rapidly changing social needs. One example is clearly the public library, which served as the university for the common person during the early part of this century. What are public libraries going to be and do for people in the 21st century? Is there a vision for the public librarian or information scientist, or is such a concept obsolete? Have public libraries, like the farmers' grange, outlived their original purpose? Are libraries institutions that need reinvigoration and a renaissance? If the answer is yes, then we believe the best way to do that is by developing people to effectively meet the challenge.

We believe that all professions and most institutions in this country represent social contracts between the people they serve and the people who are serving them. Certain rights have been given to professions and institutions. If you are a professional, you get to police yourself. You get to ask your own questions because we trust that you will ask questions that are in the best interest of society. You get to set your own agenda. That is what professional freedom means, whether you are a doctor, lawyer, or librarian. That is the freedom that people strive for. However, we feel that a lot of professions have become very narcissistic. Their questions often reflect self-interest or institutional bias more than the larger concerns of society.

The Foundation is interested in professional development in information science because we see it potentially as a critical area that could make a substantial contribution to solving social problems. Obviously there is a demand for professional service around new information systems or there would not be so much competition emerging. Therefore, our questions include the following: How relevant are librarians and library schools to the next century? Is your research useful? Is this research being synthesized in a way that allows people to use it? What is the vision driving change from within the profession? From outside the profession? Is there leadership within the area? What kind of students are seeking out the profession? How do you recruit people into the profession and develop those already within it?

We are in the process of trying to answer these and other questions. In about a year, we plan to come up with a program statement on this emerging program priority that will define the types of areas that we want to fund. This is the time for you to try to impact our process in formulating a program. Later, if the program fits with your interests, you may want to approach us with an idea for a grant.

HOW FOUNDATIONS OPERATE

Before approaching any foundation, it is very important to understand something about the philosophy of the foundation. Almost every foundation operates under some kind of philosophical tenet and set of values. These can usually be found in annual reports or in other documents. Glean those out and let them guide you in your approach.

For instance, at the W. K. Kellogg Foundation some key philosophical statements from Mr. Kellogg serve as the basis for our internal discussions and help distinguish us from other foundations. One such statement is, "I believe in helping people help themselves." That puts an emphasis on people and self-help—on empowerment processes. Does your idea relate to that process? Another important statement that I think is relevant to libraries is, "We believe in the application of knowledge to the problems of people." Clearly, libraries have a strong application of knowledge component, but how do they relate to the problems of people? Is it obvious? Can it be made obvious? Where do the needs of libraries fit with the foundation's philosophy and program goals?

Another one of Mr. Kellogg's statements is, "I'll invest my money in people." We believe that people, even more than institutions, get the job done. Therefore, we want to see people working together to solve problems they face in common. Leaders who form effective partnerships to address critical issues become a catalyst for change, and we want to help empower that type of leader. These are examples of the types of philosophical statements and program preferences that will let you know if your idea is in tune with some of what we, at the W. K. Kellogg Foundation, are focused on.

It is also important to know what type of foundation you are dealing with before you approach one. People often do not distinguish between a private foundation and a corporate foundation if it carries the same name as a corporation. If I tell someone from the Battle Creek area that I am with the Kellogg Foundation, they'll say, "Don't you hate it since they automated the assembly line?" Then I'll say, "Well, it hasn't impacted me much. You see the Foundation is totally separate from the Kellogg Company." However, because of the shared name, people often do not distinguish between us, thinking we are a corporate foundation rather than a private one.

IBM has a corporate foundation. They give away approximately $225 million a year, which is higher than our total last year. As a private foundation, we are one of the larger players, and we are growing so our opportunities are expanding. In addition to private and corporate foundations, there are also community foundations. They often raise their own endowments and take on responsibility for projects that are no longer supported by a tax base. Family foundations are often small and operated by family members as a memorial or trust. In addition to the basic types of foundations—private, corporate, community, and family—we can be distinguished on the basis of how we do business. For instance, a foundation can operate the programs it funds, or it can make grants to others to operate the program or project, or it can do both. The W. K. Kellogg Foundation is a hybrid—we make grants and also operate a limited number of programs ourselves, such as our leadership programs. It is important to know the size, type, and style of the foundation you want to approach; they come in many different varieties.

As part of discerning the philosophy and type of foundation, it is useful to know something about the founder. How was it founded? The philosophy is often tied to information related to the founding. Some foundations are tied very tightly to the founder, and some are not tied to that person or group of people at all. At the W. K. Kellogg

Foundation, we believe that Mr. Kellogg was a genuine philanthropist. We think of the Foundation as an active dynamic legacy of W. K. Kellogg's beliefs. In particular, he believed that people have the power to improve their lot in life and the culture they are living in. He wanted to see new knowledge applied to solving problems. Our grantmaking supports application and utilization of new knowledge but does not support research per se. Ideas that do not reflect these values, regardless of how good they may be, will not be a priority for funding.

Also, it may be helpful to know something about a foundation's board. How does the board operate? Foundation boards vary widely in their composition and practices and preferences. The W. K. Kellogg Foundation has a much more involved board than many foundations. Our board meets monthly and reviews every request. Many foundations do not take this sort of working approach with their boards. Our image of ourselves is tied to the characterization of a very active, working board. We think of ourselves as people who try to stay close to the ground where the practical problems exist. We try to be problem solving in our approach. Our board is formulated with that approach in mind, and we develop our strategic plan based on it. We sell the plan to the board, and then every idea we present must be rationalized against that plan for the board to approve funding. In this process, we have to justify every proposal that we seek funding for to the board. So when you interact with us or want to present an idea to us, know that our staff will always be asking, "How will this set with the board? How can we convince them that this fits with our approved plan?"

WHAT THE W. K. KELLOGG FOUNDATION FUNDS

The W. K. Kellogg Foundation is a matrix organization, and that influences the scope and range of our program priorities. We have five major grantmaking areas: education, youth, leadership, health, and agricultural and rural development.

Cutting across these five areas are additional priorities, such as community-based programming and family and neighborhoods. Leadership is also a cross-strategy. The people in our Foundation meet in goal groups. We develop strategies around each cell in the matrix. People meet from interdisciplinary programs to debate and discuss program strategies. We do not think any area should be managed solely by the experts in that field. We may put someone who is not an expert in leadership into the leadership group. We do this because we feel that the only way to break down walls and to get the kind of collaboration that we are asking of other people is to try to engage in a similar struggle ourselves. We understand it is not easy, and to hold ourselves accountable is not always easy either. Emerging program priorities are not on the matrix but have the potential for being included if they grow and develop.

The W. K. Kellogg Foundation likes to fund evaluation and dissemination activities as an integral part of a grant. Not all foundations do. We see these as a critical part of the investment. If we give a grant, we hope to learn something that may be of use to others. If we don't evaluate it, how will we know what impact the grant had and what we learned from it. Effective sharing of results is hinged on effective evaluation and documentation. We respond favorably to an idea that is well-formulated, comprehensive, and clear. We also expect ideas to involve collaboration or partnerships. Our experience also teaches us that sustainability past the funding period is important. Evaluation, sustainability, and dissemination are all forms of accountability as well as ways to leverage the Foundation's investment. Evaluation and dissemination are both growing in importance at the W. K. Kellogg Foundation. If you are approaching us with a concept or idea for a grant, it is wise to have a notion about how you would evaluate results, sustain activities once the funding is gone, and extend what you have learned to others who could benefit from it.

We receive about 9,000 proposals a year. Out of this number, we fund about 300. Many of the 9,000 proposals come from people who make 500 copies of their proposal and, after they have gone through funding books at the library, send a copy out to everyone on their list, hoping for a hit. This is not the most effective way to approach the W. K. Kellogg Foundation. We prefer that people send a brief concept paper or call us. We are happy to listen and react to an idea in light of our current and always evolving funding priorities, our value system, and other special circumstances. We do not want potential grantees to spend valuable time writing a 70- to 100-page proposal without any guidance or feedback from us.

The 9,000 applicants' proposals take a tremendous amount of review time and threaten to bog us down. Sometimes we decline a request because the project does not fit easily into any of the cells of our matrix. Or, it may be that we have already given six grants in a particular area and have expended that area's allocation for the year. Or maybe we are looking for geographic distribution, and there have been three similar ideas in the Midwest and we are looking to fund something on the East Coast this time. We can help give our applicant important feedback that would let him or her know our preferences ahead of time. Most foundations and grantmaking agencies do not operate this way. For instance, sometimes we run into problems in working with academic people. With their training and experience, they are often used to tight guidelines and to completely developing their idea prior to any feedback or interaction with the potential funder. It is really hard for them to believe that we just want a telephone call or a one- or two-page statement of an idea first—before a proposal is drafted to see if we are interested and able to entertain the idea at a more detailed level.

I recently received a proposal from the University of the West Indies where I used to work. A colleague there is interested in continuing education for engineers. They need a downlink, and he is asking for a piece of hardware. I will have to tell him we do not fund hardware except if it relates to an overall program that fits into a cell of our matrix. If you send a proposal saying you need a downlink, the answer is going to be, "That's not our priority; we don't fund technology hardware for the sake of technology hardware." It is more effective to hear that after writing one page than to have spent a lot of time preparing a grant and then hear it.

We generally do not fund buildings, either. Yet there are continuing education centers all over the United States with the Kellogg name on them. We built those buildings, not because we wanted to build a building, but because our value system believes in continuing education, a place for all ages at a university, and the strengthening of the link between society and that university. Again, our emphasis is not on the building per se but on how to encourage universities to make a commitment to lifelong learning.

As I mentioned, we fund about 300 new grants a year, so we do a lot of screening of the proposals that come to us unsolicited. We also try to seek out people who are clearly engaged in work that relates to our current priorities and goals—people who we see making a difference, community-based leaders for instance. When we ask community leaders if they ever thought about writing a grant to the W. K. Kellogg Foundation, they often reply by saying they do not think they could do it. That is unfortunate as we feel that some of the most deserving causes and innovative people may be intimidated by the grantmaking process. In some cases, we have participated in the grantwriting process all the way from outlining to acquiring technical assistance to help them write a grant. We are not just people sitting at desks reacting to proposals—we are very much involved in developing programs in partnership with grantees to achieve the goals we negotiated with our board.

In summary, I am advising you to know your audience before you draft or submit a proposal to a foundation or other grantmaking group. One of the most effective ways to approach fund raising is by conducting thorough market research before you get too far along with your idea and to develop a contact with a person at the foundation or agency who can help guide you. I have tried to give you a brief overview of the preferences of the W. K. Kellogg Foundation, but you need to learn more about us and to develop your idea within the context of that knowledge and understanding. Many businesses do market research before setting their course. If you do the same kind of thorough background work with funding agencies, you will increase the likelihood of being awarded a grant.

W. DAVID PENNIMAN

President
Council on Library Resources
Washington, DC

Funding Priorities and Funding Strategies

ABSTRACT

When planning a funding request, librarians must understand the societal forces affecting a library's parent institution and the forces affecting the library as a social system as well as a technical system. Before approaching a funding body, librarians must ask themselves whether issues that are important to them are also important to the funding body. When approaching the Council on Library Resources, specifically, librarians should be aware of four research areas of interest to the Council—human resources, economics, infrastructure, and processing/access.

INTRODUCTION

Senator Harry Reid (D.-Nev.) said, in a Senate debate on cutting the proposed 1991 budget for the Library of Congress, "We in this country have to recognize that the security of this nation, the defense of this nation, rests on more than things that explode. A secure, strong nation also depends on people being able to have books to read, to be able to gather and retain information" (Hall, 1991, p. 19).

Despite such insightful and appealing statements, we continue to see library budgets cut and operational costs increasing. Therefore, it is not surprising that library professionals interested in research look to foundations as an additional source of funds.

It is important to understand that libraries are a major financial investment in this country, despite severe budget constraints. The National Commission on Libraries and Information Science (NCLIS) estimated just a few years ago that over $6 billion was spent annually on libraries. The Foundation Center, headquartered in New York, has compiled statistics that appeared in a recent American Library Association publication on the role that private foundation funding has played in augmenting library activities (Smith & Borland, 1991). They reported the following:

- Total library funding from private foundations for 1989 (the latest year for which data were available) was approximately $72 million, about the same as in 1988. The total number of grants was approximately 500 (they reported only grants over $5,000).
- Libraries in general receive a very small percentage of total private foundation funding dollars—between 1 and 3 percent. Furthermore, grant funding is a small percentage of total library funding (approximately 1 percent).

So, the money available for libraries in general and research in particular is limited.

SOCIETAL FORCES AND PARENT INSTITUTIONS

The forces affecting the institutions in which libraries reside are also important to understand. In a recent issue of the *Bulletin of the American Society for Information Science,* Carla Stoffle (1991), reporting on a session at the annual meeting of ASIS, summarized the societal factors affecting the parent institutions of libraries as follows:

- First is the switch from a manufacturing-based to an information-based society. I would modify that to say that we are seeing a switch to a service-based society where companies are focusing on customer service even though they may still manufacture goods—often in other countries. Universities, too, are beginning to view themselves in this service-based environment from a *business* viewpoint.
- Second, she points out an increased emphasis on "accountability." Institutions are being challenged to their very core. Their worth is no longer accepted on the basis of anecdotal evidence. That was certainly true at Bell Labs, where I spent the past seven years. Characteristic of this trend, I see a new level of accountability emerging. Institutions are being asked to measure their performance and to have their leaders accept responsibility for this performance. If they do not achieve their goals, new leaders are brought in.

Institutions that were previously funded routinely are being asked to demonstrate their worth. My recent visits to a variety of institutions tell me that this trend is increasing, and it is not limited to educational institutions or industry; it is pervasive.

- The final factor identified in Stoffle's article is the changing demographic makeup of the United States. This move towards more cultural diversity is more adequately described in a report titled *Workforce 2000* (Johnston & Packer, 1987) that was issued a few years ago. It carries implications for all institutions and organizations— profit and not-for-profit—in terms of the emerging labor force and customer base.

I would add two other factors to Stoffle's three:

- First is the increasing globalization of our industries and institutions. We can no longer operate in isolation for both competitive and moral reasons. Companies and countries are no longer isolated. East and West are meeting in the marketplace as well as in political forums. And institutions such as libraries must learn how to open global boundaries as well.
- Second, a trend we can no longer deny: a shrinking economy in the United States in which even some of our most vital institutions are having to rethink their levels of spending. At the same time global economics is playing an increasing role, we see a fragmentation of Eastern Europe, the unification of Western Europe, and the continuing emergence of the Pacific Rim as a major economic force.

SOCIETAL FORCES AND LIBRARIES

If these are the forces acting upon parent institutions, what about libraries themselves? Certainly technology has played a major role in the evolution of libraries and will continue to do so even in (or especially in) tight economic times. But let me make my position clear regarding technology and its impact on our future in the library community.

We must look at our libraries as social systems, not merely technical systems, and we must act in social terms when we look to the changes ahead. Some people believe the future (especially the technological aspect of it) "unfolds" like a giant preprinted road map. Such people strive to peek beyond the folds and guess ahead about the next major event. This approach assumes a predestination that I find difficult to swallow. I believe *we* must shape the future, not let *it* shape us.

And we must realize that we are confronted with a paradox. We must introduce change—and, I believe, radical change—if we are to continue to play the vital role that libraries have played in the past.

To state the paradox simply: to remain what we are, we must change; if we do not change, we won't remain what we are.

The issues that must be addressed by all of you can be stated in concise terms:

- How to manage constant or declining funding while the costs of materials continue to rise; and
- still respond to increasing and complex demands from library users— and respond we must to maintain libraries as the vital social institution they have been.

FOUNDATIONS

You undoubtedly see parts of these issues that you want to address, and the part you want to address is important to you. But is it important to a foundation that might provide financial resources for your study? Again, the Foundation Center provides some excellent guidance. A newly issued *National Guide to Funding for Libraries and Information Services* (Olson, Kovacs, & Haile, 1991) provides detailed information on almost 400 foundations and corporate sources. It also provides a "filter" of important questions you should ask yourself before approaching the foundation:

- Does the foundation's interest include the specific type of service or program you are proposing?
- Is the foundation interested in your geographic area?
- Is the amount you request consistent with the foundation's funding practices?
- Is there any policy of the foundation that could be a barrier to your request?
- Does the foundation prefer shared funding, or does it like to be the sole source?
- What types of organizations does the foundation support?
- Are there specific deadlines or other procedures that must be followed?

Do not rely entirely on this new publication—as good as it may be, you should look at material available from the foundation itself, such as its annual report.

COUNCIL ON LIBRARY RESOURCES

Focusing specifically on the Council on Library Resources (CLR) now, I want to describe how we would suggest you go about preparing a funding request. *Before* you send in a full-blown proposal, give us a preproposal letter (or phone call).

- Discuss the general problem you want to address.
- Why is it important to you?
- Why should it be important to CLR?
- Why should it be important to other groups—i.e., are the results likely to be extensible?
- What are the general ballpark costs?

If we move on to the proposal stage, then more detail will be required, especially in the areas of assessment and dissemination—i.e., how can we measure the results to know if what was done was effective, and how can we communicate those results?

CLR spent just over $1 million last year, and I expect our new and expanded set of programs to increase the annual funding level, but let me caution you. The areas of interest to CLR in the future will be based on the strong belief on my part that we cannot continue as we are. We must be prepared to be held accountable for the benefits as well as the costs of what we do. That is true for libraries, library researchers, and yes, even CLR.

Furthermore, CLR's future work will reflect my belief that libraries must be viewed, first and foremost, as information delivery systems, not as warehouses. The dilemma is that libraries have many roles: that of warehouse, gateway, intermediary, communication channel in the scholarly process, and preserver of what we know. The major challenge must come in what we see as the driving force or motivation for libraries. For what will their leaders be held accountable? When these leaders have their backs to the wall (as many now do), what will be the essential vision and force that motivates their decisions? Will it be risk averse or bold? How will the success of the institutions they lead be measured? I believe CRL can help bring about necessary changes in this community, and I believe we can help bring about those changes with a sense of urgency that is essential.

The same questions hold true for library education and research. How will leaders be measured? I believe we must see a closer relationship between library research and the major libraries located near library schools. I believe information science, rather than being a threat to librarianship, can be a powerful ally, and we need more interdisciplinary research demonstrating this fact. I believe library educators need to place a greater focus on research—and research that is externally funded. And I believe that library researchers who are risk averse will not serve their institutions well. There is a call for boldness and urgency there as well.

Research focused on libraries can be a vital force for change. But beyond that, CLR is also concerned with the broader issues faced by related information service providers, including computer centers providing database services; university bookstores that can work in conjunction with libraries; bibliographic utilities that support library operations; and university, commercial, and professional presses that provide input to library collections, because these are all part of the interconnected world in which libraries now operate.

And that leads me to identify four general areas that I believe need significant attention and that I intend to see CLR focus on over the next few years in the form of research projects as well as other related efforts.

First is the area of *human resources*. We need to look at the end-to-end issues of attracting, educating, maintaining, and advancing individuals in the information services profession. We should not focus major emphasis on the question of what to do about failing library schools, but rather on the question of what to do to assure a steady stream of talented people into leadership roles in libraries and related information service organizations. Some specific questions I would pose for study in this area include the following:

- What can be done as far upstream as possible to attract bright young people into the information profession?
- How and when should these people receive their basic education and their first professional degree in the information services area?
- How can we assure that professionals in this arena will be able to serve the culturally diverse audiences that will make up their user population?
- What mechanisms are needed to assure that continuing education becomes a normal part of the professional's life and that the people already in the profession receive the training necessary to continue to serve their users well?
- How can mentors as well as other developmental mechanisms be used to assist in creating strong leaders?
- As leaders reach the end of their careers, what can be done to assure that their skills and experience are used to "prime the pump" and create more leaders in the information profession?

Second is the area of *economics of information services*. Over time, we need to address the full range of economic issues associated with libraries and related information services, including both micro- and macroeconomic issues. At the outset, however, I believe we should focus on microeconomic issues and, more specifically, on those questions that will lead to a deeper understanding of information service operations in libraries. We need to be able to answer questions such as the following:

- How much do we really know about the specific functions that a library performs in terms of being able to measure these activities?
- What are the unit costs of these functions, and how/why do these costs vary across libraries?

- How do these functions fit together to form information services (e.g., document delivery), and what is the overall cost of these services?
- What are the ways in which we can measure benefits of these resulting services in order to perform cost/benefit analyses from the user's viewpoint as well as from the viewpoint of the institution in which the library or service provider resides?

I am convinced that the cost and value of information services must be understood and that quantitative analyses are essential to the responsible management of libraries now and in the future. In addition, I believe that many of the tools and techniques used in the "total quality management" programs currently receiving major attention in U.S. industry are appropriate for the redesign of our information services. We need to understand more fully how these tools can be applied in the information service arena.

Third is the broad concept of *infrastructure*. This umbrella term includes the systems, services, and facilities that are drawn upon to help libraries and other information services operate more efficiently and effectively. Included in infrastructure are communication networks, bibliographic utilities, software and hardware vendor communities, and publishers. Also included as a major component of infrastructure is the current array of physical structures that are viewed as essential to information service operation—e.g., the buildings that house libraries as we now conceive of them. Questions that should be addressed in this category include the following:

- How will emerging, as well as in-place, electronic networks modify the balance of power as well as the allocation of resources among different information service segments (including the public library segment)?
- How can publishers and libraries work together via experiments that demonstrate processes of change that are beneficial to both segments as well as to the end-users?
- What alternative designs for library facilities can demonstrate a focus on service rather than structure and illustrate that form can follow function when the function is clearly understood and articulated? (For example, storefront branch libraries are an illustration that libraries need not be edifices to be edifying.)
- How can system vendors and bibliographic utilities work together when large central operations and local systems seem to be on a competitive collision course? Is there a long-term strategy that makes sense for both and serves libraries and their users well?

Although the concept of "infrastructure" is extremely broad, I believe that a few well-chosen projects can begin to move us toward a more rational environment in which both information producers and information consumers are served well by libraries.

Fourth, and finally, is the dynamic duo—*processing and access. All* processing undertaken by an information service should be for the purpose of access. The two should not be separated (just as the Commission on Preservation and Access has made the point with regard to preservation). If we look carefully at today's libraries, we find that much of the resource is consumed to support internal processes. It is often unclear how these processes directly (or indirectly) benefit the user. There are many research questions that can be addressed on both the processing and access sides that could significantly influence the cost and/or benefit of library processes. Examples of questions I believe should be addressed include the following:

- What steps are necessary to reduce the cost/time of cataloging significantly from where they are today, and how radically can the processes be revised?
- If the users were to design their ideal information access mechanism, what would it be and how would it vary across different user segments? How would it vary from what we now have (our imbedded base)?
- How would such a design change the current internal processes in libraries necessary to sustain an access system?
- What actually occurs when users "browse" a physical collection, and how could the processes be transferred to electronic access systems?
- What mechanisms help create the serendipity that occurs when a user accidently discovers information or develops new ideas in unusual ways while in contact with information resources? How can those mechanisms be enhanced—especially where physical resources may be curtailed?

These four areas—human resources, economics, infrastructure, and processing/access—represent the broad umbrellas under which specific research projects and other efforts will be launched by CLR (and I hope by other organizations as well that are interested in the evolution of information services). As I said earlier, CLR stands ready to help those who are willing to undertake the necessary (and painful) effort of redesigning the information delivery systems we call libraries. And we look forward to continued interaction with people who provide us feedback on our efforts and directions.

REFERENCES

Hall, L. (1991, April 17). Storehouses of wisdom. *New Jersey Star-Ledger*, p. 19.

Johnston, W., & Packer, A. E. (1987). *Workforce 2000: Work and workers for the 21st century.* Indianapolis, IN: Hudson Institute.

Olson, S.; Kovacs, R.; & Haile, S. (Eds.). (1991). *National guide to funding for libraries and information services.* New York: Foundation Center.

Smith, O., & Borland, A. (1991). Foundation funding for libraries. In *Libraries and information services today: The yearly chronicle* (pp. 104-110). Chicago: American Library Association.

Stoffle, C. (1991). Libraries, funding and creativity, part 1: Funding. *Bulletin of the American Society for Information Science, 17*(2), 16-18.

Contributors

J. R. BRADLEY is an Assistant Professor at the Graduate School of Library and Information Science at the University of Illinois Urbana-Champaign. She is currently serving on the Research Task Force of the Medical Library Association (MLA), whose charge is to develop a research program for MLA. Her current research project is a study of the academic knowledge taught in undergraduate and graduate programs that relate to information, including information studies, information science, information technology, and the management of information. She is editor of *Hospital Library Management* (MLA, 1983) and coauthor with Larry Bishop of *Improving Written Communication in Libraries* (ALA, 1989).

DWIGHT F. BURLINGAME is Director of Academic Programs and Research at the Indiana University Center on Philanthropy. He received his Ph.D. in Library Science from Florida State University. He was previously Vice President for University Relations for six years and Dean of Libraries and Learning Resources for six years at Bowling Green State University. He is the author of several publications, including the recent books *Responsibilities of Wealth, Taking Fundraising Seriously,* and *Library Development: A Future Imperative.*

BLAISE CRONIN is Professor and Dean of the School of Library and Information Science, Indiana University. He was educated at Trinity College Dublin (M.A.) and the Queen's University Belfast (Ph.D.). He is the founding editor of the journal *Social Intelligence.*

LEIGH STEWART ESTABROOK is Dean and Professor, Graduate School of Library and Information Science, University of Illinois at Urbana-Champaign. Her research focuses on the effect of technological change on the nature and structure of work. She also directs an interdisciplinary project on Scholarly Communication and Information Transfer in an Interdisciplinary Research Institute. Among her recent publications are "Job Satisfaction: Does Automation Make a Difference?" *Journal of Library Administration* (Fall 1990); "The

Growth of the Profession," *College & Research Libraries* (May 1989 and reprinted in *The Best of Library Literature, 1989;* and "Staff Attitudes—Conflicting Values" in *Effective Access to Information: Conference Proceedings,* Alphonse F. Trezza (Ed.). Currently Dean Estabrook chairs the University of Illinois Campuswide Computer/ Networking Committee and serves as a member of the Illinois State Library Advisory Committee.

GLEN E. HOLT is Executive Director of the St. Louis Public Library. He received his Ph.D. in History and Urban Studies from the University of Chicago. He was formerly on the faculty at Washington University in St. Louis and at the University of Minnesota Twin Cities Campus. Dr. Holt drafted Missouri's resolutions for the recent White House Conference, chairs the Missouri Library Association's strategic planning committee, and heads the committee charged with implementing the resolutions of the recent White House Conference in the State of Missouri.

DEBRA WILCOX JOHNSON is Assistant Professor at the School of Library and Information Studies, University of Wisconsin-Madison. She previously served as Associate Director of the University of Illinois Library Research Center and currently works with the Library Evaluation and Development Service at the University of Wisconsin-Madison. Her research interests center on management, evaluation, and public services, with a specialty in adult and family literacy.

MARGARET MARY KIMMEL is Professor and Chair of the Department of Library Science, School of Library and Information Science, University of Pittsburgh, where she also received her Ph.D. Her teaching includes children's literature and services as well as a Ph.D. seminar in issues in education for the professions. She coauthored *For Reading Out Loud,* a guide to reading aloud for parents and teachers, with Elizabeth Segel. She is active in the American Library Association where she served as Chair of the Committee on Accreditation as well as a member of Council. She is also active in many groups in Pittsburgh and has been cited as "A Real Pittsburgher for 1991" by the *Pittsburgh Magazine.*

KEITH CURRY LANCE is Director of the Library Research Service, Colorado State Library and Adult Education Office. He is a co-founder, past chair, and member of the Steering Committee of the Federal-State Cooperative System for Public Library Data; past chair of the Library Administration and Management Association's Statistics Section; and a member of the Public Library Data Service Advisory Committee. For the Library Research Service, he provides contracted services to the U.S. Department of Education's Library Programs Office and National

Center for Education Statistics, the American Library Association's Office for Research and Statistics, and the Southeastern Library Network (SOLINET). As an independent consultant, he has worked with the Mountain Plains Library Association; the Idaho, Missouri, and Virginia state library agencies; and public libraries in Boise, Idaho; Corpus Christi, Texas; Lorain Co., Ohio; and Monroe Co., Pennsylvania. He is a regular organizer and presenter of sessions at the American Library Association's annual conferences and speaks at graduate schools of library and information science nationwide.

GAIL D. McCLURE is Director of Communication at the W. K. Kellogg Foundation in Battle Creek, Michigan. She manages the media resources, information systems, technology, and marketing divisions. She directs the development and distribution of publications and oversees communication and efforts for the Foundation. She also engages in grantmaking related to these areas. Dr. McClure was Vice President of the Academy for Educational Development in Washington, DC. At the Academy, she was responsible for planning and implementing agricultural and natural programs. She also directed the United States Agency for International Development's Communication for Technology Transfer in Agriculture project.

W. DAVID PENNIMAN is President of the Council on Library Resources, Inc., a not-for-profit foundation committed to funding projects to enhance library operations. Before joining the Council in 1991, Dr. Penniman served as Director of the Information Services Group and, prior to that, as Libraries and Information Systems Director at AT&T Bell Laboratories from 1984. He has served as Vice President for Planning and Research for Online Computer Library Center (OCLC), where he also established the Research Department in 1978. He has worked as a research scholar at the International Institute for Applied Systems Analysis in Austria and as an information scientist at the Battelle Memorial Institute in Columbus, Ohio, where he was also responsible for the development of the BASIS online retrieval and data management system. Dr. Penniman holds an undergraduate degree from the University of Illinois and a Ph.D. in Behavioral Science from the Ohio State University. Dr. Penniman is active in several professional societies and has published over fifty articles and papers in the areas of information systems research, development, and operation.

JANE B. ROBBINS is Professor and Director of the School of Library and Information Studies, University of Wisconsin-Madison. She is the author of numerous articles related to education for and research in library and information studies. She has been editor of the quarterly international journal *Library and Information Science Research* since

1981. She is presently working on a volume with Douglas L. Zweizig on exemplary financial practices in American public libraries. The volume entitled *Keeping the Books: Public Library Financial Practices* will be published in 1992.

KATY SHERLOCK is former Assistant Director of the Library Research Center (LRC), Graduate School of Library and Information Science, University of Illinois. She served as director, project coordinator, and statistician for the Statistical Services project with the Illinois State Library for three years. She coordinated data collection and analysis projects to promote public library planning and development and served as a resource for librarians and ISL staff with special data analysis requests. A major responsibility was the production of local and statewide statistical reports, customized for the library manager. She also implemented and managed a variety of LRC research projects for academic, school, and special libraries and library systems and associations.

JOE L. SPAETH is Professor, Department of Sociology, and Research Professor, Survey Research Laboratory, University of Illinois at Urbana-Champaign. He received his Ph.D. in Sociology from the University of Chicago in 1961. His research interests include the allocation and consequences of control over organizational resources. He is currently conducting research on a national probability sample of work organizations.

NANCY A. VAN HOUSE is currently Acting Dean and Associate Professor in the School of Library and Information Studies, University of California, Berkeley. She holds an M.L.S. and a Ph.D. from the school. Her primary current research areas are library effectiveness and the management and evaluation of service organizations. She has also done considerable research on the library labor market. In the school, she teaches courses on library management, evaluation, systems analysis, and research methods. Prior to her appointment to the school's faculty, she worked for a library research and consulting firm, for a public library cooperative system, and in public libraries. She is the author or coauthor of numerous books and articles. Recent publications include *Measuring Academic Library Performance* (ALA, 1990), *Output Measures for Public Libraries* (ALA, 1987), and *Planning and Role-Setting for Public Libraries* (ALA, 1987).

INDEX

Aburdene, P., 10, 36
Action research. *See* Practitioner research
ALA Survey of Librarian Salaries, 47
Alexander, A. W., 44, 50
Altman, E., 17, 33
American Chamber of Commerce Researchers Association: cost-of-living index, 44-45
Americans with Disabilities Act: effect on public libraries, 15
Anderson, D. G., 24, 33
Applied research. *See* Practitioner research
ARL Statistics, 41
Atlanta-Fulton County Public Library: research at, 139

Babbie, E. R., 68, 77
Baker, B., 19, 33
Ballard, T. H., 13, 33
Barker, J., 10, 12, 33
Beach, C., 13, 33
Beck, S. J., 25, 33
Bender, D. R., 10, 33
Bentley, S., 44, 50
Berelson, B., 24, 33
Berkowitz, E. S., 148, 149
Berman, J. J., 15, 33
Biggs, M., 9, 33
Bishop, A. P., 8, 13, 35
Blegen, J., 14, 16, 33
Blodgett, T., 11, 33
Bolman, L. G., 6, 33, 100, 102, 116
Bookstein, A., 123, 132
Borland, A., 159, 166
Boss, R. W., 21, 33
Boucher, J. J., 43, 50
Bradburn, N. M., 71, 77
Bradley, J. R., 3, 97, 167
Brimsek, T. A., 42, 50
Brinberg, D., 103, 106, 110, 116
Brown, S., 17, 33
Bruns, L. G., 25, 33
Bryan, A. I., 24, 33
Burlingame, D. F., 4, 146, 167
Busha, C. H., 98, 116

Cain, A. H., 20, 37
Camp, J. A., 24, 33

Cargill, J., 17, 18, 33
Carpenter, K. H., 44, 50
Casey, M. H., 21, 33
Cetron, M., 10, 33
Chase, G., 58, 62
Childers, T., 8, 33, 52, 53, 59, 61, 62
Children's services. *See* Youth services
Claritas Corporation: and demographic data, 45-46
Clark, D., 148, 149
Close, F., 120, 132
CLR. *See* Council on Library Resources
Coates, J. F., 18
College and University Personnel Association: and library salaries, 43
Colorado Municipal League: and library salaries, 43
Colorado Site Selector and Electronic Atlas, 45
Colorado State Library: research efforts of, 139
Compton, C. H., 25, 33
Converse, W. R., 8, 33
Corbin, R. A., 13, 33
Council on Library Resources (CLR): and pre-proposal research, 161-162; proposal writing for, 162-163; research projects focus of, 163-165
Cowan, C. D., 68, 77
Crocker, M. K., 43, 50
Croneberger, R. B., 11, 33
Cronin, B., 3, 117, 118, 125, 130, 131, 132, 167

D'Elia, G., 9, 34
Data collection: face-to-face interviewing, 75-76; for evaluation, 60; for youth services research, 90-92; response rate, 72-73; role in the research process, 136-138; self-administered questionnaires, 73-75
DATANET PLUS, 45
Davenport, E., 125, 130, 132
Davies, O., 10, 33
Deal, T. E., 6, 33, 100, 102, 116
Diesing, P., 98, 116
Dillman, D. A., 76, 77